POLICING STRESS
ON THE
HOMEFRONT

HOW LAW ENFORCEMENT
COUPLES CAN COMBAT
MENTAL ILLNESS AS A TEAM

Dr. Jessica Burke, Ph.D.

authorHOUSE®

AuthorHouse™
1663 Liberty Drive
Bloomington, IN 47403
www.authorhouse.com
Phone: 1 (800) 839-8640

Published by AuthorHouse 02/18/2020

ISBN: 978-1-7283-1013-8 (sc)
ISBN: 978-1-7283-1012-1 (hc)
ISBN: 978-1-7283-1037-4 (e)

Library of Congress Control Number: 2019942525

Print information available on the last page.

This book is printed on acid-free paper.

To my loving, supportive husband who has always believed in me. Everything I am, and everything I have done has been because you have loved me.

To Victoria. My biggest cheerleader, my best friend, and a person who encourages me to always pursue my dreams. Thank you for believing in me and always being proud of my accomplishments.

And to my children. Being your mother makes me want to be a better person. I hope that I set an example for you, and that you always believe in yourself. I hope that I can teach you to have steadfast determination that will carry you through any endeavor you set your mind to. I love you

CONTENTS

CHAPTER 1

WHO AM I, ANYWAY?

Let me start by introducing myself and telling you why I think you need to proceed onto the next chapters. I am the wife of a police officer in California who, at the time of this writing, has been with the department for nearly 15 years. We have been together for nearly 11 of those years. So, I married a cop, unlike many women who marry men that become cops. I will talk about why that is an important distinction to make later.

I received my master's degree in psychology, with a specialization in evaluation, research, and measurement in 2015 and proceeded immediately to my doctoral program in forensic psychology. My Master's degree has allowed me to learn how to conduct and identify quality research, as well as teaching me how to interpret the results. This has become much more important in my career than I ever thought it would be. I earned my Ph.D. in forensic psychology, specializing in police psychology, 2019.

My dissertation was on police officers' satisfaction with mental health resources offered by their department. At the end of my program, I had hoped to inspire social change by encouraging departments to evaluate their provisions from a new perspective and enhance them where the need lies by having officers themselves voicing appreciation of the efficacy of particular resources. For example, the Employee Assistance Program (EAP) is different at each department. Some offer 3 visits to a mental health professional in a given amount of time, some offer 10. I figured that an officer given 10 visits is going to voice a higher satisfaction level than those who have only ever been offered three. I thought that the results of my study would encourage departments to really analyze whether what they have is enough or if they can do something else to offer more effective resources. Unfortunately, I, not only, did not have enough participants answer the survey, the balance of the sample (the descriptive statistics of the participants in the study) was completely off. So, I changed the study to determine whether or not time in service had any bearing on satisfaction in available resources. Unfortunately, again, the analysis yielded statistically insignificant results. In layman's terms, the statistics that resulted from the analysis were unable to present any real findings. Long story short, the research was really, useless. Nevertheless, the Chief Academic Officer said that my research was well-done and sufficient to meet the requirements for a doctorate. So here I am. Getting my Ph.D. was an accomplishment I am proud of and has afforded me many more opportunities to grow in my career and mission.

My mission in life has been to improve the quality of life for police officers. I was deeply affected by the prevalence of suicide of law enforcement officers. I realize that they simply aren't caring for themselves or being cared for like they should. And I wanted to find a way to teach officers how to mitigate their stress. So, I began this mission by starting to develop a resilience program before I realized that this was really, already being done. Some of my ideas were unique, but that was not going to be my defining moment. What was missing was the training of the spouses. As a spouse, myself, I have realized that there is no preparation for us. Police officers get all kinds of training to be cops. But no one is training us how to be good police spouses. No one sits us down and tells us what to expect and how to address it. No one warns us about the impact it will have on our lives and how to best support our officers, at least not with any sort of evidence-based instruction. I found that there are many faith-based organizations that will take wives under their wing and help them from a religious perspective, but the science was still missing. With my specialty being in police psychology, and my several years of experience as a wife, I determined that I could successfully design a real, evidence-based training course that would bridge the gap that is often left by the commonality of officers failing to address their mental health concerns with neither their romantic partners, nor their peers or their administrators. Police officers are dying left and right due to suicide and often spouses never saw it coming. As a wife, myself, I had encountered many wives that did not know how to communicate with their husbands, and some that had no interest in such a thing, for various reasons that we will discuss. I set out to create a training that would address those unhealthy approaches and do something unique. Instead of gearing this toward officers, I would create this just for the wives.

This venture started modestly enough, with an effort to get this training up and running for the wives of my husband's department. I had two very good ladies that were interested in spearheading that. But at the end of the day, there was a vote. The end result of that was "The board believes that this training is necessary, but we want to find someone else to teach it." 20 years of education, 3 years of dedicated study in the field, and experience as a 8 years as a wife was not enough? Or was it simply because I, somehow, rubbed them the wrong way? Either way, good luck with that. Once I lost the support of the wives of this department, I also lost the support of the department's wellness network who I had hoped would help me get this off the ground. The fact that I was not licensed as a therapist turned some people off. This is silly, however, because why would I have a license if I have no interested in conducting therapy? I could do therapy for 30 years. It still won't make me a better teacher. It seems to be a common thought process to think that a psychology professional licensed to practice therapy is more qualified than someone with real experience, education, and specialization. I will never have a license because I will never be eligible without 3000 hours of clinical training, nor will I ever have interest in providing therapy. I love to teach and provide valuable training. And a license does not make anyone better at it than anyone else. That being said, the idea that Policing Stress on the Homefront ©2017 would be a training offered to this one group faded.

Once I realized that my passion for this would be dead in the water if I did not do something about it, I decided I was going to be more aggressive. I got my business license and started a successful business out of it. Now, don't get me wrong, I was not rolling in money, by any means. I was losing more than I was putting into it. But I measured my success by how popular it became and how it quickly turned into something that interested both departments and spouses all over the country. I began privately contracting with agencies who hired me to conduct the training, as well. as organizing events on my own. Now it has grown and become the foundation for many new ideas on how I can achieve my goals. I believed that I could improve the quality of life for police officers through their homes and romantic partners.

But this very quickly evolved into a training for couples, rather than just the spouses. More and more officers began attending the training to learn how to combat mental illness alongside the spouse. While it is still very much geared toward teaching and encouraging the spouse to commit to a different lifestyle and be more communicative with their partner, the training also teaches the officers how to let them.

At the end of every class, I ask for people to fill out surveys. 99% of my participants stated they would recommend this course to others. This surpassed my expectations. I, of course like any other professional, have my critics. But I have been consistently and pleasantly surprised by the positive feedback I get after every training. And only 4% stated that the material was only "neutral" in its applicability to their life. I attribute this to the occasional fire wife or EMS wife that would attend. To maintain credibility of my training, I make no apologies for the fact that it is specifically geared toward police officers and that my experience as a "blue line wife" is a massive component to that. While I do occasionally add in some information pertinent to other first responders, I will never create new trainings that are geared specifically for other fields. I feel that the intimate touches I can add to my training as a police wife are what makes the training so valuable. I would be more than happy to help another wife develop a similar training, however. All first responders need this kind of attention.

So, that is my professional background. Would you like to know more about my personal life? Ok, I'll tell you:

I am originally from Southern Oregon, where I went to high school and spent my freshman year of college. I joined the United States Air Force when I was 20. Due to an injury, I was honorably discharged a year later and eventually ended up living in California. I now live in a tiny, one-stoplight town an hour and a half outside of Sacramento, called Valley Springs. We live here with my husband, Dan, with whom I have been with for nearly 11 years. We live on a 4-acre property on a small farm. We have some chickens, a few llamas, a few goats, a few dogs, and a couple kids. Maddox is 7.5 and Duncan is 3.5. I love to travel, both around the United States, as well as foreign countries. I spent 9 years in college and now find myself a little lost sometimes now that I am done with it. I fill a lot of that time with staying up to date on my TV shows, chasing business, and hanging out with my boys.

I suppose I should talk about my husband too. Dan has been a police officer for 15 years. After 2 years as a patrolman, he was assigned to the motor unit where he spent 12 years. During this time, he became certified in accident reconstruction, drug recognition, radar instruction, and motor instruction. He loved being a motor, but decided it was time for him to level-up. He took the sergeant's exam and was promoted to sergeant 6 months later. He, at this time, is a supervisory patrol sergeant.

I would describe Dan as being of a mild-mannered type. He can come across to some people as laid-back, mellow, reserved, and quiet. I don't think that he is really the type to be "made" for a cop. Hell, even I didn't see a man that screamed, "cop" when we were dating. But I have also seen him turn his command presence on. He is just very good at maintaining control of that switch.

Dan is a hard-worker, an excellent father, an impressive handy-man, and an amazing and supportive husband. He picks up my slack with the kids when I am travelling for work, two things that are frequent for me. And he is my best friend. I'm extraordinarily lucky to have found him. I truly wouldn't be where I am today if it wasn't for eventually accepting a date from a man who had previously given me a speeding ticket.

CHAPTER 2

BIRTH AND EVOLUTION OF POLICING STRESS ON THE HOMEFRONT

So, I already mentioned the failed beginning of this venture. I genuinely wanted to help the officers in my husband's department by helping their partners. It became very clear, very quickly that my expertise was not only not wanted, but not trusted. I believe that getting a training from a professional with 3 years of dedicated study in mental health in law enforcement, an extensive educational background, and first-hand experience as a wife, for no cost is an excellent opportunity. But my qualifications were questioned, rumors were started and spread, I received a great deal of negative feedback from both other wives, and the wellness network in the department and realized that, if I wanted to do this, I would have to do it all myself with no one's help or support. And I did. Once I put the information out there, I fielded phone calls from spouse groups, police departments, and mental health agencies to organize a training for their officers and families. I really, never imagined that my training could take off like that.

For my first training, I recall receiving a call from a wife asking if she could bring her husband. It had not occurred to me that officers would have any place in my class and I told her, "Sure, but I doubt he will want to come. It really is geared toward the wives.' Nevertheless, there was an officer in my first class and I loved the interaction between both he and his wife as learners, and as someone I could bounce my logic off of to either show that I was right about many concepts, or that I had more to learn on others. After that I encouraged officers to attend, and by my fourth class, every single participant came as part of a couple. While my training has always been applicable for the spouse attending alone, I far prefer to see the officers attending with their spouse. It really shows a willingness to have a part in their own mental health management. And it also illustrates the importance of working as a team.

When I am explaining my course to clients, I often have to go over the history of my training to really illustrate why it is so much better to involve both the officer and romantic partner. I also like to throw in some of the statistical data that supports it. For example, a study showed that % of officers surveyed stated that the supportive social interactions of their romantic partner after a critical incident was crucial to avoiding the development of PTSD symptomology (Evans, Pistrang & Billings, 2013).

80%!

This is a huge number. Yet, there are very few trainings, if any, that are geared toward helping romantic partners help their officers. Many clients just want me to work with the wives, which is fine. But I always encourage them to consider sending their officers along too. While I can spend hours teaching the spouse how to communicate better with their officers, how to understand body language, support them after a critical incident, reduce anxiety, help the officers and themselves adopt health coping strategies and deal with vicarious trauma, none of it matters if the officer is shut down and unwilling to let down their walls for their spouses to step into their world. Further, I think it is great for a couple to have something to work together on. Mental health is so important and often not appropriately tended to. What a way to strengthen a marriage than to find a common enemy in mental illness and work together to fight against it?

Yes, the officers that come to my class do often find things that they would call, excuse my language, "pussy shit." And that is okay. I am married to a cop, so I have learned to expect this logic. But I have never had an officer leave my class thinking that they just wasted their time. The beauty of my design is that I created a model to follow, but one that is not rigid. You may not agree with all my ideas and tips. If I knew the perfect way to go about it, I would be a very rich woman who everyone pays to see. But the truth is, I am not perfect and while not all my tips will work for everyone, I have yet to hear a person leave my class saying that they didn't find any of it applicable or useful. The system won't break down if you don't play my conversation-starter game, or if you don't follow the three-question rule (which you will learn about later). I designed this to be a pool of information and tools for the user to choose from in a way that best suits their unique relationship. At the end of the day, the important part is positive change. Even if a couple only implements one tool, they are making a positive change in the way they regard mental health in the home. This leads to an improvement in an officer's life. That is all I can really ask for.

In 2019, I built off of Policing Stress on the Homefront ©2017 and developed a train-the-trainer course. It became a two-day training where agencies are able to adopt the training as their own and have training officers certified in the principles teach-back the material to their own officers. It became more popular than I ever imagined, and I am looking forward to seeing how far the information spreads. As of the time of this writing, I have over 100 training officers in agencies across 11 states have adopted Policing Stress on the Homefront ©2017 as their own method to assisting their officers' families to manage their mental health in the home.

I have big dreams for Policing Stress on the Homefront. Right now, it is a really unique training that you won't see a whole lot of. I like to say that it is, "cutting-edge). I want that to change. I want Policing Stress on the Homefront ©2017 to be California POST (Police Officer Standards and Training) certified sometime in the near future. I want this training to become a common addition to the more advanced departments' mental health programs. I truly feel that making these kinds of positive changes can save both marriages, and lives. Someday, other people are going to start developing similar trainings, and I would like to set the bar for their development.

Beyond continuing on this track, I am hoping to bring my work back to my home-base and offer this training without having to fly somewhere every 2-4 weeks. I love what I do, and I love travelling for work, but the lifestyle is not sustainable when you have two children. I have also had clients ask me if I could provide them with a webinar. This idea is intriguing however, I feel that so much education is drawn from the face-to-face interactions that we share in class, that there would be a significant loss to the value. I have also considered training "satellite instructors," giving certified spouses the opportunity to travel and deliver the training for me so that agencies can still benefit from the training without requiring me to clear my schedule for it. I think there are a lot of directions this could go. Whatever happens, I hope that this training lasts a long time and continues to help lots of officers along the way.

CHAPTER 3

PSYCHOLOGICAL RESILIENCE

What do you think about when you hear the word, "resilience?" I always think about the times I have inadvertently caused my children to bump their heads or acquire some other minor injury, and hearing long-time moms say, "don't worry, kids are resilient." Resilience is one's ability to "bounce back." More specifically, it is an individual's ability to experience trauma, trials, or tragedy, and return to their pre-crisis status quickly (APA, 2019). The word "quickly" is relative. The fact that a police officer can experience something horrific today and go back to work tomorrow shows some level of resilience by itself. But is that officer really bouncing back? Often, the answer is no. He is bottling it up and doing what is asked of him. He is expected to be strong enough to handle these traumatic events. And he is expected to suck it up and go on like nothing is happening. This practice contributes to an officer's likelihood of developing PTSD increasing. An officer with solid psychological resilience not only can cope with traumatic events effectively, but he can also grow from them.

The issue with the idea of psychological resilience meaning that the individual returns to pre-crisis status quickly as it relates to police officers is that the time frame following trauma can often involve more trauma exposure. The average human likely won't be experiencing traumatic event, after traumatic event, after traumatic event like a police officer does. For example, if a person is violently assaulted on their way home from work, the chances of them experiencing another similarly traumatic event during the days following the event are very slim. Not only are their acute stress responses liable to cause them to avoid situations that seem remotely dangerous, it is simply not common for a person to experience massive trauma back to back like that. However, a police officer might see a gruesome dead body on Monday and get shot at Tuesday. This is why psychological resilience is so important to police officers. In order to negotiate that effectively and to come out on the other side unscathed, an officer must be able to cope with trauma, return to pre-crisis status quickly, and grow from that trauma accordingly. But psychological resilience is not something that is trained as a rule at the moment. It is a luxury provided only by the departments that have budgets and philosophies reflective of a perceived necessity to enhance their mental health resources. Psychological resilience can be learned and developed by anyone. But we must make this type of training more normal for law enforcement training environments. The stigma on mental health is an obstacle that stands in the way.

When I teach about psychological resilience, I also teach about the General Adaptation Syndrome. This is what happens to our resistance to stress when a stressful event occurs:

Right now, sitting quietly on the couch or laying in bed reading my book, you are in a state called, "homeostasis." Your resting heartrate is somewhere between 50 and 70 beats per minute or so give or take 20 beats, I suppose. Your stress hormones are manageable, you are not good are bad, you just…are.

Then you hear the sound of breaking glass coming from the other room. You are startled and there is a dip in your resistance to stress. Your heart races, your adrenaline starts pumping, your adrenal glands start releasing massive amounts of cortisol, which is your stress hormone, and your energy suddenly increases.

You grab the nearest adequate weapon and approach the sound as your resistance to stress is leveling back out as soon as you gather your wits about you and start to get control of your racing thoughts.

As you approach the broken glass, you see a strange man standing inside your back window and you instantly recognize an imminent threat, causing you to spring into action. This is where you are approaching the peak of your resistance to stress. The question is, what choice do you make? Do you run? Do you hit the person with the weapon you picked up? This is your fight or flight response, or adaptation. This is when you are adapting to stress and have decided what you need to do to survive. Your body starts to repair itself so that you can make a decision. Everything starts to level back out, but you remain in an alert stage to decide how you will defend yourself.

You decide to fight. You engage the threat and eventually win the battle. The man jumps back out the window and runs away. Now you your resistance to stress will do one of two things: it will return to homeostasis, or it will sink to exhaustion. The outcome depends on the psychological resilience of the person. If you have healthy psychological resilience, you will return to homeostasis, or your pre-crisis state.

Now, let's apply this to an example more suited for a police officer's situation.

You're patrolling your beat. There is currently no threat. No calls are holding. You're just driving. Your heart rate is normal. Your breathing is steady.

Suddenly, you hear a panicked voice on the radio, "Shot's fired, I'm hit!" As your cortisol skyrockets, your heart races, and your natural inclination is to take short, shallow breaths. Your blood is deoxygenating, you're getting a little shaky, and you start playing through possible scenarios as you race to the scene.

You get there, jump out of your vehicle and immediately have to make a decision. Do you engage the threat and fire your weapon? Do you take cover? Do you run? Do you tend to the officer's injuries?

You decide to engage. You neutralize the threat, and you have adapted. After the you have gotten past the initial stage of shock, realizing what has just happened, your heart race starts to decrease, your cortisol levels start to decrease, your adrenaline starts to wind down, and you will either, return to homeostasis or become exhausted.

Now we will add a different level of complexity to your resistance to stress. Police officers live between the alarm stage and the resistance stage. Each hairy call triggers your alarm, and you are forced to adapt, just to be triggered by another call that you have to adapt to. Once you get into this habit of being constantly stressed out, your body can't cope as well, and it becomes harder to return to homeostasis. Instead, you reach the exhaustion stage.

Once you have reached the exhaustion stage, your body becomes depleted of all your physical, emotional and mental resources, and your body is no longer able to fight stress responses. This is where fatigue and burnout syndrome, and mental illness live. Prolonged exhaustion is where death lives. This is your stress-induced heart attack, or your mental illness ending in suicide. The outcome depends on your psychological resilience.

So, what factors are involved in psychological resilience? There are five main factors, and I will put them into context for both officer and spouse: The first is the capacity to make realistic plans and the ability to carry them out. For any person, this is simply one's ability to make and achieve goals. It is important that a person can avoid feeling stagnant. This could look like hoping for a promotion and eventually achieving that. For the spouse it could look like their own career aspiration or, like many police spouses, raising children, being able to pay for their college, and seeing them through adulthood. If you have no goals, then there is never any accomplished feeling that is necessary to move forward happily in life. I suspect that many people that are born into a life of luxury where everything is handed to them experience depression due to lack of psychological resilience. What fun is life when you don't need to strive for any accomplishments? You should always want more. It does not have to mean that you aren't grateful for what you have. It just means that you are motivated to constantly be working towards improvement of some sort. You should always have goals. Think of how you feel when you make a checkmark on your to-do list? It makes you want to make more checkmarks, achieving more goals. And the more short-term goals you achieve, the more likely you are to achieve your long-term goals.

To illustrate this, in my class I have the trainees do an activity. I ask someone to tell me two-short term goals, and one long-term goal. Almost every time, I get two short-term goals like, "I want to lose weight," and, "I want to go back to school." The long-term goal is often, "I want to retire to (insert state here)." What they don't realize at the time is that they are giving me three long-term goals. The purpose of this exercise is to show that, no matter how short your short-term goals are, you can break them down to make them even shorter and more achievable. If you have long-term goals disguised as short-term goals, they will sit there in space as, "one day...I will lose weight..." and you will never get there. So I have them write down a question:

What can you do today?

The answer is often something to the effect of, "Well, I could meal prep healthy meals for the rest of the week" or "I could go run a few miles or go to the gym." And then I encourage them to break down their long-term goals into several short-term goals. If your long-term goal is to buy a house, then several short-term goals could be to secure a real-estate agent, get a pre-approval for a loan, check house listings, check your debt-to-income ratio, pay off bills that will get in the way of approval, look into selling the house, take pictures, make a list of deal-breakers, interests, and requirements of what you want in a home. Every goal can be broken down into things you can do today, this week, or this month. These goals are vital for psychological resilience.

A person with a positive view of themselves and confidence in their strength and abilities is essential for psychological resilience. A police officer that views himself as a good, effective law enforcement officer, who is confident in their ability to do their job well is going to be massively more resilient than an officer who lacks confidence and self-esteem. Unfortunately, a cynical, negative outlook is an occupational hazard in law enforcement. Almost all they deal with is negativity, you can't really blame them for becoming cynical when that is what nearly 40 hours a week is devoted to.

As a partner, we can encourage this factor by making a point to facilitate increased confidence, positive self-talk, and reminders of the officer's strengths and abilities in his or her job. It is also important that the partner reminds themselves of their confidence and strength. Positive self-talk is always hard for officers to swallow because it is, there again, "pussy shit." But reminding oneself that you are good at what you do, that you're strong, and capable is important to being able to cope with the trauma that is certain to come in this line of work.

To become resilient, one must also avoid dwelling on things they cannot change. We have all done it. We get ourselves stuck in this state of disappointment and stagnancy because we have our heads and hearts set on achieving a goal or acquiring something that will never come to be. It could be a marriage ending and having a tough time accepting it. It could be losing your career and failing to accept that you have to change your career aspirations. If you fail to accept a loss or an unmovable obstacle, you stunt your development. The fastest, most realistic way to growing, is accepting that you can't change what is already lost.

Another factor is having skills in problem-solving and communication. This is one of the main tenets of Policing Stress on the Homefront. Communication is often lacking, which we will delve more into a little later.

But it is important to realize that solid communication in a law enforcement relationship is key in combatting mental illness. Think of the term, "bottle it up." This is a pretty common practice for police officers. But our bottles are only so big. They will eventually crack under the pressure. No human being can sustain the harboring of strong emotions and trauma like that for very long. It either comes out in effective communication, or it comes out in some other ugly, unhealthy way. But what is certain is that it will come out sometime. To avoid this looking like violence, and angry outbursts, or some other negative coping strategy, it is so important that both officer and partner hone their communication and problem-solving skills to respond to the daily trauma officers are exposed to. Avoiding the practice of "bottling it up" is a great start to building psychological resilience. You must have the ability to manage strong feelings and emotions, and you achieve this by communicating about and solving problems.

Being able to adjust one's interpretation of events is also a factor of psychological resilience. A component to this factor is to avoid castastrophizing. This is the biggest opponent to maintaining a positive outlook, and one reason we tend to have a hard time returning to pre-crisis status after a traumatic event. We all do this, some of us more than others. Here is an example of catastrophizing:

"OMG, my blow dryer is broken....I just got out of the shower, my hair is wet, and I can't dry it...now I have to air-dry it and its going to be a big frizzy mess...I have to be at a training in an hour...My client is going to think I'm weird because I have crazy hair...she is going to be thinking of my crazy hair the whole time...She is going to think that I am so weird that she won't want to bring me back...I am going to lose this client...My business is going to suffer... because my blow dryer broke...."

We have to avoid thinking of the worst-case scenario in every hiccup we encounter. You can turn any molehill into a mountain if you let yourself get away with it. Some people are so skilled at catastrophizing that they can turn even a positive into a negative. The more we cater to these irrational thoughts, the harder it will be to bounce back when something bad happens.

Finally, post-traumatic growth is essential to developing psychological resilience. Post-traumatic growth is one's ability to learn and grow from trauma. In order to move past an event, a person must be able to reflect on it, glean from it, and apply what one has learned from it to move forward. Here is a story to illustrate post-traumatic growth:

So, when I was about 19 years old, and a freshman in college, I met a guy who quickly turned into a very abusive boyfriend. This went on for about 6 months. Before this happened, I didn't really know where I wanted to go in my life, but law enforcement was not even a blip on my radar.

One night, after being punched in the face a couple times, I finally decided that it was time to call the police. That is when a deputy from the Jackson County Sheriff's Office in Oregon came to my rescue. Watching this deputy put this man in handcuffs changed my life and sparked a new interest in me. I thought, "Hmm…maybe I want to be a cop…"

I was too young for that, so I joined the JCSO's explorer post. For those who don't know what that is, it is a group of young adults and teenagers who have an interest in law enforcement that volunteer to aid the police department in a number of ways. I thoroughly enjoyed my time with them and decided, yes, I do want to become a cop.

I was still too young, however, as I was only 20 by this time. So, I joined the Air Force and, after graduating basic training, attended the 343rd Security Forces Training Squadron which was essentially the police academy. I made it about halfway through when I suffered a career-ending injury and was honorably discharged, learning that I would never be able to be a police officer. My stubborn self said, "No. Somehow, someway, I am going to be a cop." This mindset continued for 4 years. I spent that time screwing around in law enforcement classes in college, working jobs that were really just intended to support me until I could be a cop, and constantly being sad that being a cop wasn't working out for me.

Finally, in 2009, I realized that I wasn't going to be a cop. It finally dawned on me that I needed to consider a new career field. I decided that I was interested in linguistics. I started learning Arabic and thought that maybe I could work oversees as a civilian contractor in military operations. I went to the VA to collect on my educational benefits and was told that they would not fund my training. My case manager handed me an aptitude test and said, "take this test and wee will see what we can do."

Whatever I scored high in, it suggested to my case manager that psychology was the way to go. He said, "I'll tell you what. I can get you approved for funding IF you go for your bachelor's degree in psychology." I said, "I don't want to do psychology," I said. "Well then we aren't going to pay for your college."

"So, where do I sign up for psychology?"

3 years later, I received my bachelor's degree. I decided, maybe psychology isn't so bad. But you can't really get a job in the field if you don't have, at least, a master's degree. So, 2 years later I got my master's degree in psychology with a specialization in evaluation, research,

and measurement. By the end of that program, I decided that I hated research. And, unless I wanted to suck it up and find work in the research field, I needed to go a different direction. 4 years later, I earned my Ph.D. in forensic psychology, specializing in police psychology. I met Dan right before I started my bachelor's program and by the time I discovered police psychology, I already had nursed my old passion for law enforcement back to life. It was then that I realized that I wanted to aim my career toward battling mental illness in law enforcement.

This was not all sunshine and rainbows for the entirety of those 9 years. There were hiccups, tragedies, trauma, 2 babies, 2 traumatic birth experiences, 4 house moves, several bridges burned, financial hardships, a major car accident, and periods of marital strife. Any one of these trials could have broken me down and encouraged me to quit. But I was determined to achieve my goals this time.

In 2017, I developed Policing Stress on the Homefront ©2017 and within a year, I was training the Jackson County Sheriff's Office in psychological resilience. I had gone full circle, and reached where my passion was born.

Now, do me a favor, read my story again and circle every part of the story that illustrates all the factors of psychological resilience that we have discussed in this chapter. You will find several points in the story. I'll wait.

...

...

...

Great job! So, you should have circled the moment I realized that I wanted to pursue a career in law enforcement after being beat up by an abusive boyfriend. This is post-traumatic growth.

You should have circled, 2009 when I accepted that I would never be a cop and decided to pursue a new field. This was me accepting that I couldn't change it. I dwelled on it for 4 solid years and wasted a lot of time and energy in the process. Once I made that decision, it was only up from there.

Maybe you circled the positive outlook I maintained through 9 years of major life events that threatened to knock me down. It is not easy to achieve goals. But those achievements are sweetened by the sugar that is obstacles that are overcome to do so.

And you probably circled the moment that I came full circle to train the agency where I got my start. I remember driving around the town, initially experiencing sadness and a little anxiety from passing landmarks that reminded me of my trauma. But then I realized how far I have come not only since then, but *because* of it. This is post-traumatic growth.

Psychological resilience is so important in our lives. If it's arguable, I would argue that it is *most* important in our lives. Life comes with trauma, no matter who you are. We all have to know how to come back from it to survive.

CHAPTER 4

EXISTING LITERATURE AND RESEARCH IN MENTAL HEALTH IN LAW ENFORCEMENT

Over the course of my doctoral program, I have had the pleasure of reading hundreds of articles on mental health in law enforcement officers. I also have had the privilege of working with professionals who help me sort through all of it and learn what is important about police officers. So, when I designed Policing Stress on the Homefront, I pulled out some of the most important studies to illustrate the importance of changing your lifestyle to best mitigate work-related stress.

First, I want to discuss prevalence and stigma. There are lots of studies that suggest varying statistics for mental health issues. But of the ones I have seen, it would appear that the number of officers that meet the diagnostic criteria for mental health conditions like depression, anxiety, and posttraumatic stress disorder (PTSD) reaches up to 40% (Fox, et. al.,2012). What we, in the field of research, have discovered is that police officers are inherently deceptive when being questioned about mental health issues, even when offered conditions of anonymity.t being said, it is expected that results are underreported, suggesting that these numbers are higher than what is yielded.

I think it is important to talk about prevalence, mostly to reduce the effects of stigma. Perhaps, if officers realized that what they suffer from is pretty common, they would be more likely to speak out and/or address their concerns. The fact that prevalence is so high confuses me because stigma on mental illness is such a huge obstacle when nearly half the population deals with mental illness. Normally, we see high stigma attached to low prevalence, and high prevalence attached to low stigma. I like to use medical analogies to work toward changing the way we perceive mental illness. Take Aids verses the Flu. The flu is pretty common. We have all experienced the flu. Lots, and lots of people have the flu at any given time during flu season. We very easily go get our flu vaccines. We don't get all shy about requesting one. We pretty freely tell people we have the flu. In fact, many people are quick to put it on their social media accounts. The prevalence is high. But the stigma is low.

Now, if you have AIDS, you're going to act quite differently. You will be very selective in who you tell. You may be embarrassed to have to say it out loud, lest someone hear you. It's definitely not going on social media, and we may feel a lot of shame to be diagnosed with this illness. The prevalence is low. The stigma is high.

So why is that discrepancy present in law enforcement? It's an anomaly that can be attributed to the long-standing police culture that says mental illness is a weakness. We must break this cycle. Police officers die because they are afraid to ask for help.

Another study I found is on supportive and unsupportive social interactions following critical incidents. This is one of the first studies I read and, also the catalyst for the development of my training. This study was the first I read that highlighted the importance of the romantic partner in coping with trauma. The study found that most police officers say they benefit from their romantic partner's support after a critical incident (Evans, Pistrang, and Billings, 2013). So, why is it so uncommon in law enforcement families? We will answer that question in a bit.

Another study I read and reference in my training is one conducted in 2013 by Conn and Butterfield. They surveyed officers and developed a list of both helping and hindering factors that contribute to mental illness and a police officer's ability to cope with trauma. I like to reference this study because I think it is an eye-opener to spouses who do not truly appreciate the gravity of what their officers experience. This brings me to a small tangent off the point for a moment. I recently read a post on a police wife page that mentioned that her husband was getting training for mental health to learn how to decompress. She said, "who helps me decompress after a long day with the kids?" If this is your thought process, either close the book now or proceed with caution. You may not like how I feel about that kind of statement. At the end of the day, unless your children are leading you to dead bodies, or causing some other kind of unusual trauma that is known to lead to posttraumatic stress symptoms, or you find your stress comparable to trauma, or if you find your stress comparable to your officer's trauma, then I apologize but you are part of the problem. I am not saying your mental health is not important. Skip to my vicarious trauma chapter if you don't believe me. But you do have to understand what repeated exposure to trauma does to a person. That is why this study is included in the training. It is so important to understand all the factors that are involved in the development of a mental illness in law enforcement officers. Let's take a moment to discuss each one.

Among those factors were:

Self-Care

Self-care is really any coping strategy that involves activities that a person does for themselves to manage stress. Officers in this study mentioned time-outs, naps, hobbies, exercise, faith-based activities, and many others. Taking care of oneself is of obvious importance. However, these types of coping strategies are often not seen. I like to get my hair and nails done on a regular basis. Some officers like to maintain a healthy exercise and nutrition routine. These are self-care strategies.

Family/Significant Other Support

This is the part of the study that highlighted the benefit of a police officer having a supportive partner, just like the previous study. These results that came directly from the thoughts of police officers show without a doubt how important it is to be a supportive partner when he or she is repeatedly exposed to trauma.

Talking with Co-Workers

Support from peers is extremely important, but it is often nowhere to be found. Due to the heavy stigma on mental illness, especially in this field, officers don't talk to each other enough about their mental health concerns. This can be attributed to fear of termination due to mental illness, or harassment in the form of bullying if the wrong person gets the information. But this study shows that support from peers would help in reducing the vulnerability to PTSD. It is vital that officers bond with other officers so that a trusted friend is close by for help when it is needed.

Emotional Engagement

Imagine for a second, that you are on an airplane. During the safety briefing, they remind you to put your oxygen mask on before assisting anyone else with theirs. Why do you suppose they have that rule? Well, because if you pass out from lack of oxygen in the process, you're not much help to anyone else. But, what if the person next to you was your small child? Would you still follow the rules? Most mothers and fathers say no. Well, this is very much like policing for some officers. They believe that emotional engagement is a necessity to be a good cop. So, they engage with victims and, perhaps, criminals and try to find relatability in them, or even hope for something better. The problem is, it requires energy, and like oxygen in the mask, if you are using it for someone else, you're going to pass out and eventually burn out. Energy in emotional engagement for police is very similar. You can't pour from an empty cup, so eventually that tendency comes back around to hinder recovery from trauma. While I am not saying that officers should stop engaging, I am saying that this is something that needs to be understood and addressed by adopting healthy coping strategies.

Work Environment

This encompasses a number of things. It can be related to the citizen to officer ratio lending to how busy the call log is. It can refer to the state of equipment, relationships with peers and administrative entities. The environment the officer works in plays a massive role in his mental health and ability to cope. Efforts need to be made to level it out. Some are out of the officers' hands, but adopting healthy coping strategies is key.

Mental Health Resources

Some departments are making big steps toward enhancing their mental health provisions. But others are falling victim to a lack of attention to the issue. I have seen departments that have a long way to go but also are making big strides. And I have seen departments that have lacking mental health programs, if any. But these provisions are so important to an officer's likelihood of developing mental illness. There is one department I know of that implemented their program 5 years ago or so. They are extremely proud of it and have been awarded for it. They start with new rookies in the academy and implement a day totally dedicated to mental health. They check on them later and make sure to reach out when they have experienced trauma. Here is the problem, the veterans and officers with over 5 years are being all but ignored. I know of two officers that were first responders to a suicide by train where the head was completely severed. Two rookie officers responded to the scene toward the end. Later, the mental health team called the second two officers to see how they were doing, but the older, more seasoned officers that responded first were completely ignored. This is an example of a department that has good intentions but is still failing their department. While rookies are likely to experience their first critical incident within 3 years, officers with 5, 10, 15, 20 years of experience have certainly experienced a great deal of trauma over their whole career. Police departments must have good Employee Assistance Programs, they must tend to ease of access issues, they must break down the stigma.

Personality of the Officer

Of course, this will be different for every person. Personality encompasses a variety of things that determine how a person navigates trauma. This is both nature and nurture. Many components of our personality are innate, and many are influenced due to a number of life experiences. This has an impact on how officers cope with trauma later. Further, psychological resilience is important here. Some are more resilient than others as part of their personality, which will have an impact on their ability to cope.

Ability to Help Victims

I've never met a cop that got into law enforcement because it is such a lucrative career. Most officers do it for the opportunity to help others. This is great, but this career does not afford officers this opportunity all the time. Almost every cop will experience a desperate attempt to save someone without yielding fruitful results. Other times they will want to help someone, and their hands are too tied to do so. This wears on an officer over time.

Relatability to Victims

I like to use the example of Officer Smith and Officer Johnson when explaining the importance of understanding how relatability to the victim plays into development of

PTSD symptoms. Officer Smith is a single, unmarried man with no children. Officer Johnson is married with a 3-year old. A call comes out on the radio of a drowning of a 3-year old. Both officers respond to this call and try to save the baby, but are unsuccessful. Who do you suppose is more likely to develop PTSD? Officer Johnson is going to see his child's face on that baby's body for the rest of his life. And that will be a trauma that is difficult to overcome. Officer Smith will, of course, also suffer distress from this call. I don't know a single cop that won't say that children are the toughest to cope with. But the relatability is tough.

Remember I mentioned a major car accident? About 3 years ago, I was in a bad roll-over car accident with my 4-year old and 4-month old sons. I was exhausted and shouldn't have been driving. I only was because my 4-year old was very sick and I needed to take him to the doctor. On our way back, I fell asleep and careened off a highway, rolling my vehicle over an embankment. The kids were fine. I had a concussion, but it could have been so much worse given any other elemental change. A year later, I ran into the officer that responded. He told me that, at the time, he had a 4-month old baby and we, at the time, did not know if Duncan, my youngest, was fine yet. He was relieved to hear that he ended up being okay but admitted to me that he had a really tough time coping with the accident. We had never met, but he saw his baby's face on my terrified baby's face after what could have easily been a fatal vehicle accident.

And relatability is not just a reference to children. Cops find relatability every day. They see their grandmother's face on the old lady that got scammed, or their sister's face on the young lady that was raped. They see their troubled brother in that 15-year old that is on his 8th ride to jail. It is essential that we understand how this contributes to coping with trauma.

Scene Reminders

What is the difference between a combat veteran with PTSD and a police officer with PTSD. Answers may vary. Some would say there is no difference. I disagree. Now, bear with me and hear me out. Now, this is not to trivialize combat PTSD. It is often extremely severe, and the *quality* of the disorder is comparable to that of police officers. But the *experience* of it is not the same as what police officers experience. A combat veteran generally leaves his home and is placed in a war zone for anywhere from 6 months to a year. In that frame of time, he experiences dead bodies, explosions, children hurt or killed, getting shot at, losing friends, killing people, and just a sense of constant fear for their life. Then they come home to a relatively normal environment. They are still susceptible to scene reminders, but as a rule, many of those scene reminders are only seen on the battlefield and not on the front lawn. Police officers are repeatedly exposed to trauma and then spend the next 10, 15, or 20 years being exposed to the scene reminders. Those reminders could be something as ubiquitous as a brown truck, an above ground pool, a certain bank, or a particular intersection in a road. This makes it a little more complicated to treat, in that there is no way to limit exposure to triggers without them coming off work. Again, adopting health coping strategies is key.

Continued Exposure

In this study, continued exposure referenced the amount of time an officer is exposed to a traumatic event. Studies show that exposure to human remains and watching someone die are perceived to be very intense for many officers. Unfortunately, when they are exposed to this, they don't have the luxury of walking away. Often times, they have to stay with the body, or go over what they witnessed again and again. They may be asked to make a notification and be present when the family is experiencing heartbreaking emotions over the loss of their loved one. They may have to be questioned later, then again at trial, then again on the first anniversary of the event, etc. Every moment that an officer is exposed to trauma, the synapses in the brain are strengthening. We will talk more about that later.

Exposure to Human Nature

Most of us have Facebook, and being married to a police officer, I subscribe to a lot of police pages. That, unfortunately, also means that I see a lot of horrible news stories that are shared on those pages. I might click on that story about the mother who did something terrible to her child. And I might get chills over what a monster she is, but I have the luxury of clicking that little X in the corner and walking away from it, sure to forget by the end of the day. An officer does not have that luxury and experiences everything they can't show you on television. He sees the body, the blood, the weapon, the mental state of the mother after killing her child, the sorrow of other family members, and a renewed understanding of what people really are capable of. In the study, an officer spoke about a call where an infant was sexually assaulted. He said the worst part of it was just the realization that a human being was capable of such a thing. The officer was deeply affected by the newfound understanding that his fellow humans were capable of this type of evil. These are things as wives we do not really think about. What is this job doing to your officer? And what can you do to help?

Vulnerability of the Victim

In psychology, we have four vulnerable populations: children, mentally ill, disabled, and the elderly. As a rule, these are the populations of victims that officers deal with most often. Abused children are among the most difficult of calls a police officer has to respond to. Seeing helpless or defenseless people being victimized wears away at an officer's faith in humanity, making him more susceptible to mental health concerns.

Presence of Additional Stressors

This factor in the study referenced the various stressors that an officer may experience outside their work. This could include marital problems, financial problems, issues with their children, and any other stressful event that occurs in the typical human's personal life.

I like to use this study in my training because, for the spouses, it opens their eyes to the wide variety of factors that contribute to their officers' resilience, or lack thereof. It's not just the trauma of an awful scene or an officer involved shooting. Its that, and everything leading up to and away from it.

I have known wives to say, in response to a conversation about PTSD and other mental illnesses, "Well, my husband has never seen anything traumatic. Just regular things that a typical cop experiences, so I don't think he really has a problem with PTSD or anything like that." What they don't understand is that a police officer can go through a 20-year career, never having drawn his weapon, or even experiencing a hugely traumatic scene, and can still have PTSD.

I also like to show the officers that are attending that whatever they are feeling is normal. They aren't the only ones that get heart palpitations when they pass an above-ground pool on their beat after that drowning baby call last week. They aren't the only ones that feel empty at the end of their day because of emotional engagement draining them. This is part of reducing the stigma. We have to normalize mental illness and help-seeking behavior. We are sympathetic to the average joe who experiences trauma. We don't chastise a rape victim for feeling scared to walk home at night, or a domestic violence victim who cries because a random stranger yells at her. So, why is it so hard to accept that officers deal with trauma all the time and they experience the same cognitive processes? I think that we expect cops to be able to "handle it" because "its part of the job, it should be normal to them." But they are human and are not any more fit for trauma exposure than anyone else. Yet, the stigma on mental health is so bad that over 50% of officers say that they would consider a diagnosis of a mental illness a personal failure and attributable to weakness. But what they are experiencing is completely normal. This mentality is probably why over 200 police officers died by suicide in 2019.

Another interesting study I read involved officers' ranking of critical incidents by individual perception of intensity. Before we go on, I want to explain what "critical incidents" are. In conducting literature reviews for my research, I found a discrepancy between the police department's definition of critical incidents, and what can be found in the research. A critical incident, as explained by your average police department is any incident, essentially, that invokes the loss of life of either an officer or a citizen. This could be an officer-involved shooting, an in-custody death, or some other major crisis. But the research considers such activating events as watching someone die, exposure to human remains, failed resuscitation, and interviewing child victims as significant critical incidents (Chopko, Palmieri, & Adams, 2015). This is important because it often means the difference between offering resources and ignoring officers completely. Peer support teams will sometimes make a point to reach out to officers whom they know have experienced a rough call, but they usually aren't insisting upon seeing the department shrink, and some departments don't have peer support programs. So, officers experiencing really rough calls often are dismissed.

In this study, they asked officers to rate the intensity of each critical incident. I found this study interesting because it demonstrates how different cops can really be from one another. Some officers felt that watching someone die was the most intense while others reserved that score for officer-involved shootings. I usually bring this study up because I believe it is important for a partner to know where their officer ranks these incidents. My husband is pretty stoic. He manages his stress very well. After 15 years, he has become pretty desensitized to much of the negativity of police work. I know where he would rank exposure to human remains on this list.

About 12 years ago, my husband responded to a four-vehicle collision in a well-known intersection. Nobody was wearing seatbelts and almost everybody died. Most of them were decapitated in the crash. My husband said there were literally heads rolling on the ground. He was also one of the first officers I spoke of earlier who had to deal with the suicide by train. I have learned that I do not need to encourage him to talk to me every time he experiences these critical incidents (as outlined by the research). So, I won't pry. But I know that, if he comes home and mentions a severed head, I need to key in and press a little. I know that while he does not have a problem with dead bodies, as he has seen dozens upon dozens, severed heads kind of wig him out. Other cops have more of a problem with dealing with victims of child abuse. Every person is different, and it is helpful for the partner to have a good understanding of how their officer is affected by typical police-related events.

The last study I bring up is a Violanti (2004) study on suicide ideation in police officers. I save this for right before a good break, but I also tend to use it for the purpose of opening the eyes of the partners to what the possible consequences of failing to navigate this lifestyle with mental health in mind.

In this study, 115 officers were polled anonymously and asked if they had ever considered committing suicide. A whopping 27 of them said yes. That is 23% or nearly one in four. At this point, I usually apply the math to the population sitting in my classroom. "There are 30 officers here. 6 of your husbands have considered committing suicide. There are roughly 800,000 police officers. 23% of that is 184,000. These are massive numbers." I also mentioned that, as a researcher, I have to consider the fact that this number is under-reported. Even when promised anonymity, it is to be expected that some will still claim to never have experienced suicidal thoughts.

Last year, more officers died by self-inflicted gunshot wounds than those that died at the hand of felons. Let's do some math. In 2017, 59 officers were killed by either gunfire or some other type of assault (ODMP, 2017). According to Police Magazine, 140 officers committed suicide in 2017. That means that police officers were 2.3 times more likely to kill themselves, than to be killed by someone else. This says that mental illness is a bigger killer than bad guys. If they aren't talking to each other, and they aren't talking to a therapist, and they aren't talking to you, who are they talking to?

I will end this chapter with a story I read from an anonymous post on a police enthusiast page of some sort.

The officer telling the story goes down to the locker room, mid-shift on a hot day. He saw another officer that was taking off his shirt and vest. He says, "Hey that's a good idea. It's so hot today, I think I'll take mine off too." While doing so, he gets involved in a conversation with the guy and they end up exchanging contact information and becoming friends." A couple days later the guy calls him from a roof top. He says, "I've got a couple beers, want to join me?" He says, "Sure! That's a great idea." So, he goes up to the roof, sits with his new friend, and they chat for hours. A few days later, the officer finds out that the reason the guy was taking off his shirt and vest was because he didn't want to get brains on them when he ate his gun later. And when he called from the rooftop, it was because he was standing on the ledge and was scared he would jump if he was left alone.

I tell this story because it illustrates the need for officers to check in with each other, and for partners to check in with their officers.

CHAPTER 5

EMBRACING THE LAW ENFORCEMENT LIFESTYLE

I kick off every class with an activity where everyone gets to say a few things they are hoping to learn from taking my class. Without fail, there is always one person who says, "I want to learn how to leave work at the door." And I always say, "Then you're in the wrong class because I don't teach that here."

Police officers do not have the luxury of the ability to get off work and actually be *off work*. They are cops 24/7/365. The rigorous training they go through, the activities of the day, the trauma exposure, and the nature of the job all ensure that he is carrying it with him at all times. So, it is unrealistic to expect them to walk in the door and pretend work is not still on their mind. They are remembering the smell of the body they sat on or wondering how a citizen complaint will shake out. They are always on guard and looking for evidence of trouble. Any good police wife knows that you never sit facing the door when you go to dinner with your officer. They cannot shut it down. And they should not have to.

I believe there are 5 reasons that law enforcement couples don't communicate about work as often as they should:

1.) the officer doesn't want to talk about it, so he bottles it up.
2.) the officer feels like he is protecting his family by not discussing it.
3.) the spouse does not want to violate the sanctity of her home by discussing the negative qualities of the job
4.) the spouse does not want to be reminded of the danger.
And 5.) some combination of all of the above.

But talking about work is necessary! And it does not have to be all negative. But it does need to be addressed. And I will have you know, I have talked to wives that say, "oh yeah! He tells me everything!" Meanwhile, the officer admits that he doesn't share everything with her for fear of hurting her delicate mind in some way.

So, we have to try to embrace the job at home, and this can be hard for some spouses. In my class, I use a graphic which is a swat team, seconds before barreling through a closed door. This is my warning for those wives in attendance that make a habit out of pretending their husbands aren't cops. By committing to this new lifestyle change, it may feel a bit like a whole lot of death and destruction pouring over your threshold. IF you're not used to hearing about what goes on during a typical work week, this could feel like a violation of that sanctity she has created. But it is absolutely vital that we become okay with it. Cops rarely talk to therapists, and they hardly ever talk to their peers. So, we need our home to be their safe space to talk, their soft place to fall. Their sanctuary. You, as the partner have a phenomenal opportunity to help your officer stay afloat in a sea of trauma.

Let's talk about what "sanctity" and "sanctuary really mean.

A "sanctuary" is a place where one can go to rest and recover." When my husband gets home from work, I prepare my shoulders for a heavy burden. This is what I believe it means to be a true partner. I want to experience what he is experiencing. I want to help him carry that. He can come home, let go of his burdens a little, rest, and recover. While it may be logical for a wife to consider the death, evil, and hatred that often accompany "shop talk" as directly counter-intuitive to the idea of sanctity, my husband being able to come home and open up about his emotions and experiences is what makes our home a sanctuary for him.

Now, if this is not a common practice, it can be difficult to get the ball rolling on this level of communication. My best piece of advice is to find ways to make light of his work. I, personally, love when Dan tells me funny stories from work. I have grown to favor cop humor over all other kinds. So, I adore when he tells me funny stories. It might be about a bimbo that hit on him, a naked drunk guy he had to fight, or even the odd way a body was positioned. Who knows? But it makes things a little easier. And let's talk about morbid humor. It can be off-putting for sure, but it is a solid, and truly beneficial defense mechanism. You have heard the saying, "If I didn't laugh, I'd cry......"

Another important way to embrace this lifestyle is to make a point to talk about the scarce positivity of the job. We will talk about that more in the next chapter. But the point is to not dwell on the negative aspects of the job, despite the fact there are more of them. Your house will become a gloomy place if you only talk about the negative parts of the job. Talk about the time he felt proud, happy, content, or excited about his job.

The bottom line is that you will not survive on pretending your husband is a doctor. It serves no good purpose. The rest of the book is not supposed to be just a bunch of psycho-babble. It is meant to convince you that you must make a commitment to form your lifestyle around your spouse being a cop, and not in spite of it. What I mean by this: we do not have normal lives, so why do we try so hard to pretend we do? Why do we refuse to talk about the reality?

As spouses, we are the first line of defense against mental illness. We play a vital role in determining whether or not our officers will develop depression, anxiety, or posttraumatic stress disorder. And I understand what is being asked of you. But now is the time to make a change. It is a sacrifice to make if this lifestyle is not congruent with your principles. But our officers make sacrifices every day. This is only a small sacrifice to make in return.

CHAPTER 6

OPENING AND MAINTAINING A HEALTHY DIALOGUE

Of all the things I teach in my class, most of it boils down to effective communication. None of it will work if the communication aspect just isn't there. We start with what I call, "the initial discussion." I stress in my training that this isn't a lifestyle change the spouse just makes on her own and he follows suit. It is a negotiation of terms. The two parties come together, discuss what has been learned, what tips they feel comfortable with, and which they feel are inappropriate for their unique relationship. The spouse, ideally, agrees to always have a listening ear, while the officer agrees to be open moving forward. At the end of the discussion, the couple should be able to move forward with a flight path that they have both mutually agreed upon for the purpose of better managing mental health together. Like I said, this is not meant to be an all-or-nothing structure. Take some of it, take all of it. Either way, any one of these techniques can improve your relationship.

Another major component of the initial discussion is discussing the "what can I do?" aspect. If you are currently married or in a relationship with a cop, you may have already experienced that moment where you are just beside yourself and don't know what to do. This often occurs after a critical incident where the spouse simply does not know how best to support her officer after trauma exposure. That is a heartbreaking feeling that can sometimes be prevented by a preemptive strike. Asking your spouse, "when you're feeling this emotion or that, what can I do to help you feel better?" before there has even been a need for knowing the answer makes you mentally prepared to effectively support your officer after an incident. The answer might be a hug, sex, food, space, quiet time, a nap, or any number of things. When the time comes for that initial need for support immediately following trauma, the spouse is prepared to offer the things that she now knows her husband needs to start returning to a pre-crisis state.

Likewise, the partner should ask, "what should I avoid doing?" This gives the officer an opportunity to say, "when I feel ABC emotion, I really don't like it when you do XYZ." It is incredibly difficult to figure out what to do when our partners are struggling. Especially as it relates to trauma exposure when we want to offer support the most. The helplessness a partner experiences when they aren't sure what to do for their officer is a heartbreaking feeling. Taking a strike against this requires a good plan in place.

The most important component to this is that the spouse agrees to be open to discussing details and issues of the officer's job, even those that might make her uncomfortable. This will also include that spouse's limitations. In my experience, the limitation is usually, "I want to hear about your experiences, but I can't hear about the children." While these limits are important to clarify, I also encourage pushing those limits when it becomes a struggle. For example, child calls are often the most troubling for officers. So, it is not beyond the realm off possibility that when your officer needs you the most, it will be because he wants to talk to you about a dead child. This is when I encourage the spouse to really look within herself and find a way to circumvent the vicarious trauma. Maybe the answer is to say, "I can't hear about the kid, but tell me what your feeling and let's work through your struggle." Or perhaps the spouse will be sympathetic to the need to talk, that she lets down her guard. Every couple will be different.

Just as important, an officer must be willing to agree to being more open. Trust that your spouse has the mental fortitude to support you and give her the benefit of the doubt. Let your partner decide what he or she can handle. Both parties need to be willing to push their limits and widen their boundaries.

After the initial discussion, and an agreement has been reached, it is time to start executing the techniques.

Back when I started getting serious with my husband, I made up the "three-question-rule." I have used it every work-day for 10 years. When Dan gets home from work, I ask him 3 questions:

1. How was your day? – His answer to this is almost always good, fine, it was work, or some variation of that. I am never trying to get him to break down and bear his soul when I am asking him this. This is just me saying, "I am open for business." This starts the flow of conversation and lets him know I am engaged. This is not where the magic will happen.

2. How many tickets did you write? – My husband was a motor officer, so traffic enforcement was his primary job for the first 9 years of our relationship.

Listen. I don't really want to know how many tickets my husband writes. The reason being: Dan's motor-mode sounds like a real asshole. One time he gave a seatbelt ticket to a double amputee. This man had no hands! I don't need my image of my husband sullied by being reminded that he makes people miserable for a living. My husband would make a 98-year old grandma walk home in the rain if he found out her tags were expired. Okay, he probably isn't quite that bad. He might call her a cab. Nevertheless, I ask him because I do want him to know I am interested in the details of his job. This eventually lets him know that this is something that is okay to talk about and gets him in the habit. It started with an answer like "26 and no warnings" and now is more to the effect of, "26 and let me tell you this one story..."

3. Did anything interesting happen today? Is this where the magic will happen? Still no. At best I get, "not really." If I am lucky it will be a good story about a badge bunny or fighting with a man in his underwear, or some other laughable story. But at worst, I might get a, "it was a rough day, we can talk about it later." Again, this is to further demonstrate that I truly have open ears for what he is experiencing at work.

After years of practicing this, I truly believe this is one of the main foundations for our open communication about work. I believe that this rule created a conditioned response over the years. It was maybe silly at first, but he grew to realize that I really do want him to be open. Me saying, "I want to hear what you have to say," was not a disingenuous way of voicing support, rather I really meant what I said. He has always understood that it was my way of checking in with him and reminding him I am listening. And I have always been truly interested in what he has to say.

The question game is something else I made up, which is something that we do not do very often. But I have found it can be the catalyst for many of good conversation. The game involves each party asking 3 questions. 2 are unrelated to work, and the third is. So, an example of this would be, "What was your favorite subject in high school? What was your favorite childhood memory? And tell me of a time you experienced fear at work." Sometimes he will say, "I don't remember." But often this is the beginning of a deep conversation that can involve some emotional output. It gives us an opportunity to really discuss what emotions he has that are associated with trauma exposure. Other questions might involve anger, frustration, or distress. I also will sometimes ask about the more positive sources such as happiness, pride, or contentment.

It is important to talk about the negative emotions, but it is equally important to discuss the positive ones. Officers experience seasons in their commitment to the job. Right now, it is a rough season for cops. The divisive media, political changes, and racial tension is making it a difficult world for police officers to be happy where they are at. So, it sometimes helps to remind them why they are here in the first place. Talking about a time they changed or saved a life helps to renew that positive energy and rejuvenate the love they have for their job.

Whatever you do, make sure that when you play this game, it is at the right time. We do this when the kids are down for the night, or when we are on a long car ride. The reason this is important is because you simply do not know what will be yielded from such a conversation. It might not be anything. But if it is something, you do not want any distractions. The last thing you want is the kids interrupting a fruitful discussion involving a strong emotion.

It is also essential that you make yourself available. This is easier said than done sometimes. Dishes can wait, kids' schedules can be shifted, house can be cleaned later. But a police officers' interest and willingness to speak about trauma will expire as quickly as it developed. My husband knows that if he has an emotion to discuss, I will drop what I am doing to listen. I will never tell him to hold on to it while I get some other nonessential task done. I will tell the kids to wait, I will do dishes later, I will clean house later (if at all. I hate cleaning.), and I listen to what he has to say. Resolving difficult emotions as a result of his trauma is the number-one priority.

Which brings me to my next, often controversial point: you have to learn to hold off on your own issues. Unless you are a first responder of some nature, you are fairly unlikely to have experienced trauma in your average day. So, while your mental health is just as important, you are not likely to have anything to discuss that should take precedence over his trauma exposure.

In order to get on board here, you need to understand the difference between stress and trauma:

One day, I woke up at 6:00 am, an hour I try really hard to avoid, because my 3-year old stood in front of me, showing me 2 pieces of bread, asking for a sandwich. Meanwhile, my autistic 7-year old was throwing a holy fit because whatever electronic he was fixated on was not working. The dog was having one of his crazy fits and running back and forth while I wiped the sleep from my eyes and gathered myself. During the crisis, I completely spaced a conference call with an east-coast potential client. That didn't go over well. That agency never did hire me.

By the end of the day, one fire after another, I was exhausted and stressed out. I was frustrated, and a little emotionally beat-up. I looked forward to unloading on my husband once he got home from work. Stress

However, my husband also had a rough day. He had to go on a search-and-rescue mission for a severed head, as it disappeared after being separated by a passing train. Trauma

Trauma trumps stress. Every. Single. Time. This is not to say the spouse's mental health doesn't matter. It truly is just as important. Please don't walk away from this book thinking that Dr. Burke says the only mental health that matters is that of the police officer. However, I am saying that someone has to talk first, and if the difference is between stress and trauma, then trauma goes first. Stress can be discussed later. Nothing you talk about will ease the stress. But discussing the aftermath of trauma can make all the difference in the life of a police officer moving forward.

Now, if today was a little different and you got mugged on the way to work, by all means, let him have it. But when a police officer has a "bad day," that could mean that he saw a dead body that disturbed him, had to notify a family member of a particularly tragic death, or almost didn't make it home.

At this point in the training, there is always one woman who takes offense to this logic. I always coax that person out of the group and have them repeat back to me what they heard me say. It is always some variation of "you're saying he is more important than me and I am supposed to be a good little housewife that plays the submissive role." And I always say that is not what I am saying. But trauma has to be prioritized. We can't get into the habit of allowing his emotions and trauma exposure to fall by the wayside or to avoid processing and decompression. His decent days are often worse than my worst days with respect to exposure to trauma. So, it is necessary for me to allow him the first right of refusal on talk time. My waiting ten minutes, or an hour to talk about how much the kids drove me crazy today, or the stressful day I had at work is not going to leave me with an increased risk of developing a mental illness. But failing to address difficult emotions may.

Now, while my philosophy on this suggests encouraging discussion about trauma, it does not involve forcing the person to speak. There will be times when he is just not in any position at the moment to discuss it. Ideally, you will have already had a conversation about a lifestyle change and negotiated in promises to work on communication. However, even if an officer promises to be more open and communicative, it doesn't necessarily mean it is easy. There are times when the situation simply doesn't allow for an emotional discussion. An officer may need a little time before he is ready to break down and talk. As the spouse, this can be difficult to navigate. While it might feel right to say, "please talk to me! You promised!" or some variation of that, it is important to be able to recognize when you need to stop. Many psychologists believe that you can treat trauma without having the client relive the trauma by going over it again and again, and that forcing recall can increase their chances of developing PTSD. We want to avoid triggering them or making it worse for them. During the initial discussion, it helps to find out what kind of cues you should be looking for to recognize when it is time to back off and try again later. For me, it is when my husband is kind of short and irritable with me. Once we get past that, we can have a good discussion. But when I see that, I might say, "ok, I think we need to talk about this, but let's try tomorrow." Then tomorrow, I will probably check back in with him if he seems like his behavior has changed. Sometimes the officer will just say, "I don't want to talk about this now." And honestly, I cannot promise that every officer will eventually break down and spill. But that doesn't mean you shouldn't continue to encourage him to open up. It is just essential that you find the balance between encouraging and walking away. If you do walk away to give him space, always come back. Don't just let it fall by the wayside. He needs to know that you are willing to give him space but are serious about being more communicative.

I will generally reopen the dialogue when I can see any kind of change of behavior within 24 hours. If I feel like he is devolving, or if he seems like he is in a better mood, I will check in with him again. Whatever happens, I will *not* force him to recall his trauma. Its one thing if he comes to me to tell me the details. That's okay. But its another if I push him so hard that he feels like he is forced to relive what he experienced. Forced recall is *never* an appropriate form of communication.

Once being more communicative becomes a consistent part of your lifestyle, it will also be less awkward and more relaxed. You will notice you will not have to try so hard to get conversations going. Things become more fluid and natural when you have built trust, understanding, and both have expressed a willingness to practice good communication. After years of practicing this, it is not uncommon for my husband to approach me and say, "So, I have an emotion!" This is usually silliness laced with an inclination to discuss something with me.

CHAPTER 7

COPING STRATEGIES FOR THE OFFICER

Adopting healthy coping strategies in this life is key for both officer and partner. Police officers are exposed to things that many average citizens may never experience in a life time. They are human just like everyone else and need to find a healthy way of managing that. The average citizen who is involved in a traumatic event will go to counseling. Police officers, however, may experience dozens of traumatic events and never set foot in a shrink's office. I believe this is because, over the years, between the media sensationalizing in television, stigma, and the social dynamics of law enforcement we have started to believe that police officers should be able to naturally cope with trauma, because it is there job and they're supposed to be tough. I also believe that the apparent lack of adequate mental health resources provided to police officers stems from that logic. "So, you saw a dead body, you're a cop. That's normal for you." While it is normal for cops to experience traumatic events, traumatic events are not normal to the human system. The stress hormones still increase like a normal human, neurons fire like a normal human. Normal human emotions are felt. I believe that the prevalence of mental illness in law enforcement is not just related to the repeated exposure to trauma, but also to the fact that they are expected to go on like nothing happened and are discouraged from seeking help or even discussing it. I feel that this impairs the person's ability to heal.

Awhile back, I had an officer volun-tell his spouse to go to my class. He told me that he felt that she didn't understand what he goes through. I told him that understanding by the spouse often comes from the demeanor of the officer. You go to work and you experience trauma all the time. Then you come home like it was just another day at work and seem fine. It is sometimes hard for the spouse to grasp that there is a problem when your behavior isn't asking for comfort or compassion. While I am a huge advocate for wives taking more responsibility in their officers' mental health management, I do also realize that the officers can make it kind of difficult for them to do so. This is why my class is so much better suited for the couple than just the spouse.

One day, my husband's department lost a retired officer to a hit and run. My husband was the first on scene and essentially watched a man that he had known for a long time die in front of his eyes. I was aware all day that this had happened, but when my husband came home there was nothing visible that should have alarmed me. He was acting no different than any other day. He was not acting like a normal human does when they just watched someone die. He was, however, acting like a normal cop after watching someone die. It is confusing to a spouse. After a while, I had become desensitized to the fact that he is repeatedly exposed to trauma and still acts like a normal human that is not. So, I missed it in this case. A few days later he was being a complete asshole and I called him on it. He jumped down my throat and said, "maybe because I just watched a friend die right in front of me! That was a turning point for me. How did I miss this? Well the answer is because he did not come home crying about the traumatic experience he just had. He did not ask me for comfort or sympathy. He didn't ask for anything. He came home, had a beer, ate dinner, watched TV, and acted the same way I suspect a plumber or stockbroker would. This is when I learned to resist becoming desensitized to the fact that he experienced trauma every day.

For the most part, I have noticed that my husband copes with trauma very well. He has experienced what most would call traumatic on many occasions but has done very well after the event. I attribute this to his coping strategies, particularly those involving his projects and hobbies. We live on 4 acres. As far as I can tell, his hobby appears to be collecting junk and occasionally tinkering on it? He likes to collect and work on old trucks, and he likes to run the tractor to make more room for what appears to be more trucks. I truly believe his good mental health can be attributed to both his coping strategies and our open communication. With that being said, I have taken to encouraging this behavior which I find unusual.

What my husband does with his trucks and tractors…and motorcycles…and the occasional random engine, is an example of a self-care coping strategy. This is in the same category as exercise, taking time outs, napping, reading, or other activities one gets themselves involved in. These self-directed strategies are so important because they are proven to be helpful, and do not require anyone else's involvement to engage in. These are things that officers can always fall back on without anyone's help. When the counselor isn't available, when the wife isn't home, when the kids are at school, when friends aren't available, these are strategies that the officer can still engage in.

If you are the religious type, which I am finding a very large portion of LEO families are, faith-based coping strategies are also known to be very helpful. Prayer, and attending church services or church functions are excellent coping strategies. Mass, confession, bible study, extra church services, whatever is attached to your spirituality and religion, these strategies should be considered.

What comes along with faith-based practices is the idea that the world is much bigger than the officer and the spouse. It is also a source of hope and comfort that is unique and cannot really be achieved via other strategies. Now, with that being said, if you are not the religious type, I am not saying that faith-based practices will necessarily help for you. This is not me trying to pressure anyone into religious practices. I like my system to be based on scientific evidence. But there is evidence to suggest that faith-based coping strategies are effective.

A study I mentioned earlier focused on supportive social interactions after a critical incident. Almost as important as the interactions with the romantic partner were the interactions with peers. It is important for a person to have someone relatable to talk to. A cop can talk to a therapist all day long, or his wife, or a family member and there will always be one thing missing. They simply cannot relate to what officers encounter unless they, too, are police officers. So, while these people are important to talk to, it is equally important that officers spend time with other officers. It is extremely helpful for officers to speak to other officers about trauma. However, due to the stigma on mental health, this does not happen as often as it should. The fear of appearing weak, coupled with the fear of negative repercussions on one's job prevents officers from opening up about their mental health concerns to their peers.

Dan has this one friend, whom we shall call Matt. They are very close friends and he will often come over for a visit. As soon as he walks in the door, he will say something to the effect of "We're not going to talk about work. We're off work, no work-talking." I'll be damned if every single thing they talk about is work-related. Code-talking, shop-talk, the citizen complaints, the weird calls, this one-time last year…

I roll my eyes, but I secretly love it. I know that the bond they are fostering over their job is valuable. When either Matt or Dan experience trauma and need someone who gets them, they have each other.

Some departments have developed peer-support networks where officers can call upon their peers who often have received extra training. However, these networks are often linked to brass at some level. There is usually a sergeant who answers to a lieutenant, creating a perceived threat for officers who think that opening up about their feelings will get back to administrative bodies who will fire them due to a mental health concern. While visiting agencies around the country, I have found that some peer support teams have really great practices to protect their officers who come for peer support. No notes are taken, no names are written down, no proof that anything was ever discussed. In some places there are laws protecting that practice, almost as attorney-client privilege. If questioned, a peer support member can say, "I have no record of ever having talked to Officer Smith." The only exceptions to this rule are if the officer states that he or she is considering suicide, harming someone else, or committing a crime.

And what kind of a mental health professional would I be if I did not insist on considering therapy, despite the fact that it is, for most officers, an unlikely coping strategy? Employee Assistance Programs that most departments have give officers the ability to choose a therapist unattached to the police department where there is complete confidentiality. These visits are generally fully covered financially for a set period of time. However, some departments are very limited in what they will cover. For example, some may only cover three visits. Well that is like telling someone they expect them to get better in three hours. It doesn't really work that way. Other departments offer ten visits which is better but still limited. I have heard of others being essentially unlimited as long as the therapist is willing to sign off on separate issues needing therapy. This allows for an officer to get all the help he needs with no attachment to the department, alleviating the fear of repercussions. This counseling is generally also made available to the family as well in many cases.

CHAPTER 8

SLEEP HYGIENE

Adequate sleep is another major component to healthy coping. Sleep deprivation is one of my favorite things to talk about. Anyone who has ever had a baby knows what chronic sleep deprivation feels like. Some call it "mom-brain." You walk around like a zombie for several months and God only knows how you function enough to keep a newborn baby that depends on you, and you alone, alive for any length of time.

We used to think that sleep was a passive activity. We figured our brains were dormant, and that nothing was going on in there. We now know that isn't true at all. When you are getting adequate sleep, microglial cells are working hard to clear the brain of waste that is building up on the surface each day. Sleep is a restorative process and it is essential for coping with trauma experienced in the day. These beautiful little glial cells are responsible for you waking up refreshed and ready for a new day. But when you are chronically sleep deprived, glial cells called, "astrocytes" devour the synapses that are responsible for communication in the brain. As a result of this over time, neurocognitive deficits like Alzheimer's disease or dementia become an issue.

33% of police officers sleep less than 6 hours in a 24-hour period (Fekedulegn, et al., 2017). Shift-work is notorious for creating chronically sleep-deprived employees. The long-term problems with this are endless. Chronic sleep deprivation increases the risk of cardiovascular disease, metabolic disorders, gastrointestinal disorders, cancer, depression, anxiety, and even suicide. Did you know what else causes all these things? Being a cop. The minute an officer hits the streets, he is at an increased risk for these health problems. So, pursuing adequate sleep is of the utmost importance.

You know what else sleep deprivation causes? Less focus, slower reaction time, slower decision-making, slower problem-solving, decreased operational response, and poor judgement. Why do you think this is a problem for police officers? Yes! It is an officer-safety issue! Sleep deprivation is also known to contribute to fatigue and burnout syndrome. Good, healthy sleep patterns will help you act quicker, shoot straighter, take control of a scene faster and better, and help you make split-second decisions.

My husband is going to be moving to night shift at some point in the near future and he once told me, "On my long weekends I am going to stay up and get on a normal schedule and then the day before I go back to work I will go to sleep early and…."

"No. you will not do that, actually."

This is not a healthy means of living with a night-shift schedule. Your body needs some regularity for it to allow itself to fall asleep and stay asleep every night. If you are constantly confusing your circadian rhythm, you will not sleep, and the little sleep you do get will not be restful.

Part of sleep hygiene is respecting your circadian rhythm, which is your biological sleep cycle. You cannot expect to get good sleep if you're constantly confusing your body. It takes up to 48 hours for your body to adjust after messing it up like that. So, despite what your days off look like, it is important to go to sleep and wake up at the same time every day. Your body needs to know what day time is *for you,* and what nighttime is *for you.*

It is also very important to make your sleeping area as inviting and conducive for restful sleep as possible. If the officer is a night-shifter/day-sleeper, black-out curtains are a must. Eye masks are also very helpful to conceal that extra light that comes out of the corners of where the curtains meet the walls.

Some studies are showing that cooler temperatures in the room promote quality sleep, so ensure that the room temperature is to your liking. White noise has also been known to help some people sleep. A fan is sufficient for some, others install apps on their phone that create extraneous noise. And of course, we want to make sure the room is quiet from those sounds that will disrupt sleep as much as we can.

In my class, I am often asked by a spouse, "my husband refuses to prioritize sleep, what can I do to change that?" We can try, and try, and try, but we can't force anyone to sleep. But we can shorten the "honey-do" list so that sleep becomes more of a priority. We can help make the room an inviting place to sleep. And you can try to reduce any stimuli that cause restlessness like the television, the sounds of kids playing, music, or appliance sounds.

If you are the "oily" type, you can also use essential oils to promote restful sleep. Lavender, and Vetiver are known to promote sleep. Petitgrain and Marjoram are good for nightmares. And Black Pepper, Cedarwood, Melissa, and Frankincense are good for anxiety.

Another sleep hygiene tip is to use the bed only for sleep and sex. This practice trains your brain to realize that, when we are in bed, we are sleeping. So, you should not stay awake in bed for more than 15-20 minutes. But what about sex? Well, you should be fine, since sex doesn't usually last that long, does it?

Sex is the exception, not only because that is just the ideal place to do it, but also because it is an activity that promotes good sleep itself, just like getting good exercise. In addition to that, if you get into the habit of having sex before falling asleep, then this activity triggers your brain to get ready for sleep at the end. It is essentially training your brain to shut down because, "Oh! We're having sex now, sleep is next." So a more routine sex-life can be beneficial. You're welcome.

Finally, adopt a good bedtime routine. Maybe a warm bath 90 minutes before bed time, a cup of chamomile tea while you read your book for 15-20 minutes, after you complete your beauty regimen. All of these things are your act of taking control and saying, "we will sleep when I am finished with this routine. And we will sleep well."

Sleep better, be better.

CHAPTER 9

ALCOHOLISM IN LAW ENFORCEMENT

Another study I like to reference when teaching about alcoholism is one that found a link between officers using alcohol as a coping strategy and PTSD symptoms (Menard & Arter 2013). It is important to take note of the studies that illustrate a commonality on the way officers cope with trauma.

Yep, we must talk about this. I don't know many cops that don't drink alcohol a little or a lot. And I am not here to say that alcohol is inherently bad. In fact, my social anxiety is so bad, and I am so socially awkward, that the first thing I do in a social event is search for the bar to get some liquid courage. I like the social butterfly I am when I am slightly inebriated.

Alcohol becomes dangerous when one makes the connection that it is an *effective* coping strategy, albeit unhealthy. Alcohol relaxes us. It is a depressant, and there isn't anyone on this planet that couldn't benefit from the relaxation that alcohol has to offer. However, when you use it as a coping strategy, to remove painful feelings and memories, the likelihood for alcoholism and PTSD goes way up.

Officers have rough days all the time. And I am not necessarily opposed to a drink here and there to wind down. It becomes a problem when an officer says, "I am hurting right now, so I am going to have a drink. Now I feel better. This works." This is a problem because tomorrow, when he is still feeling bad, he will have another drink because it has been proven to work for him. Only now, he needs more than one drink. And this carries on. What we are not doing when we are drowning our sorrows in alcohol is getting appropriate help.

PTSD and alcoholism have a way of feeding each other. Once an officer has experienced trauma and has started to drink as a coping strategy, he is likely not seeking help, ensuring that he develops PTSD. As the PTSD gets worse, and tolerance increases, the alcoholism becomes worse, in turn, making the PTSD worse.

And this is why I recommend abstaining from alcohol for 30 days after trauma exposure. I know, I know, it seems like an overreaction, but hear me out. Let me explain stress response; For about 30 days after a traumatic event, we exhibit what I like to call, "normal, abnormal behaviors." These behaviors and symptoms are very similar to what we see in PTSD. The only real difference is that one is a temporary condition if treated correctly, the other is a manageable chronic condition. This is called Acute Stress Disorder (ASD). It is normal to experience ASD. But if you have these symptoms for more than a month, you're likely going to meet the diagnostic criteria for PTSD.

So, we have an officer that was just in a shooting who is having trouble coping with having been forced to take a life. He has gotten into the habit of drinking 1, 2, or 3 beers after a stressful day at work. He realizes that the numbing effect is pleasant for him. He isn't feeling the emotions, he isn't having panic attacks. He is sleeping at night. But soon enough, 3 isn't enough and it becomes 6. But it is still working so he doesn't see a need to seek mental health care. 30 days of this passes and now he meets the diagnostic criteria for PTSD (APA, 2013). And since he probably still doesn't have a therapist, his alcoholism is continuing and feeding his PTSD. Meanwhile, his PTSD is getting worse and fueling his chasing of the numbing effect he no longer gets from drinking 6 beers and he has graduated to harder forms of alcohol. PTSD and alcohol are dangerous together because they feed into each other's motives. The alcohol prevents the officer from realizing he needs adequate health-care, while the PTSD is temporarily soothed by the alcohol. Each one begets the other.

Further, it is not healthy to stifle your natural emotions. It is healthy to feel those emotions and have the capacity to express and manage them. If you are feeling hopeless or frustrated and you refuse to process those emotions, they will eat you alive and come out in the form of something ugly. It could be an angry outburst, intimate partner violence, or excessive force. I know that winding down with a glass of wine or a cocktail is tempting, but really think about how it is going to impact you moving forward.

So, instead of falling into this cycle, avoid the alcohol and just use this valuable timeframe to feel and process emotions in a healthy way, to stay clear and collected, and to seek mental health care. I call this time, "The Golden Hour." I truly believe that the first 30 days after trauma exposure is critical.

So why is alcoholism so common among cops? No cop is immune to occupational stress. Every cop can fall victim to fatigue and burnout syndrome. That coupled with the long-standing cultural norm that alcohol was that thing you just did after work on a regular basis as a cop makes it pretty hard to avoid. "Lock it up! They'll take your gun and badge! Just go have a beer!" was a common response to an officer struggling with a tough call. I think they called this, "Choir Practice."

I also want to talk about the dangers of alcoholism in excess for someone with PTSD. But first I want to talk about the brain's involvement in the issue. Alcohol consumption effects the prefrontal cortex by decreasing its efficiency. The prefrontal cortex is responsible for super important functions like reasoning, judgement, decision-making, social control, and problem-solving. The more we drink, the less efficient this structure of the brain is. This results in ignoring the cognitive surround. In other words, it causes tunnel vision. If you ever have been drunk you know how excess alcohol makes it hard for you to make good decisions, solve problems, or control your social choices. But this is dangerous for a police officer with PTSD who drinks frequently.

When a drunk person with PTSD ignores their cognitive surround, they can lose touch with reality (Sharps, 2010). For example, something in their house can remind them of something they experienced during a traumatic event. And with enough trauma mixed with enough alcohol, this reminder can become very real to them. This is called, "dissociation." It is triggering to an officer because, in these moments, he could very well feel like he is experiencing it all over again. He is often alone when he is drinking, so there is no one there to talk him back into reality. Alone, isolated, scared, confused, this officer will likely engage in dangerous behavior. I believe that many suicides of officers are preceded by dissociative events. At the least, it triggers panic attacks, because emotions and memories can be so strong and vivid in the moment.

As a spouse, it is important that we recognize the signs of problematic alcohol consumption in our officers. As officers, it is important that we recognize the signs in ourselves. I think that it is much more difficult for an officer to realize that he or she has a problem with alcohol than it is for the spouse to witness it.

These are the classic signs of problematic alcohol consumption:

Increasing quantity and/or frequency of alcohol consumption

Withdrawal from normal activities

Extreme mood-swings

Failure to adopt healthy coping strategies

Drinking alone or in secret

Choosing alcohol over other responsibilities and obligations.

If you or your loved one is exhibiting signs of problematic alcohol consumption, especially if there is a presence of mental illness, seek help and put an end to it before it becomes a bigger monster.

CHAPTER 10

VICARIOUS TRAUMA AND COPING STRATEGIES FOR THE PARTNER

Mental health professionals, particularly those responsible for working with trauma victims tend to experience vicarious trauma as a result of processing their clients' trauma. That being said, part of Policing Stress on the Homefront ©2017 is asking the spouses to process their officer's trauma which means it is vital that the spouses manage their own stress appropriately. Even the best therapists have their own therapists.

The spouse's mental health is just as important, and just as delicate as their officer's. And if they are entering their officer's world to hear about all the death and destruction that can be law enforcement, it is vital that the spouse stays on top of her emotions and is honest with herself about the signs of vicarious trauma. It looks a lot like depression: withdrawal and isolation, over or under eating, being easily startled, diminished joy, and difficulty expressing emotions.

Make sure you check in with yourself regularly. It can be easy to dive into this new commitment and forget about maintaining your own mental health. Ask yourself each day, "Am I okay?" Do you notice yourself feeling sad more often? Have you lost interest in your hobbies? Are you losing or gaining weight? If the answer is yes to anything, then you should probably consider seeing a therapist.

I think it is also really important to work toward fostering an identity outside of your role as a police spouse. Not everything has to have a blue line on it. You don't always have to be a police wife first. Identify as a mother or father. Identify as a lover of art. Identify as an athlete, or a good friend. Find something important to you outside of your career as a police wife and nurse it.

What would you say to someone who is obsessed with chickens? They have chicken stickers on the back window of their car. Most of the shirts you see them wear have pictures of chickens or amusing quips about chickens. All they ever talk about is their 37 chickens, how often they lay eggs, what their names are, and which one is their favorite. They show chickens at the county fair, coach 4-H helping kids show chickens, and attend all the chicken conventions. And who can forget their business embroidering cute shirts with chicken insignia?!

Sound like someone you know? Whether you say it out loud, or have an internal dialogue about it, you're probably going to think that this crazy person needs to branch out a bit.

Adopting healthy coping strategies is the biggest key to managing vicarious trauma. So, here are some thoughts on that:

I believe that it is essential to have one or two other police spouses as friends. Let me tell you a story. I used to have a friend who was not married to a police officer. One day, an officer in a neighboring county was shot and killed in a particularly horrible fashion and it hit me harder than it usually does. Maybe it was because it was literally close to home, maybe it was just the fashion in which he was murdered. Either way, I was struggling.

I got on the phone with my friend and said, "did you hear on the news about the officer in Stanislaus County?" She said, "yeah I did. Sad. So, what time are you coming over?" I stopped for a moment and was taken aback, wondering where the comforting words were, where was the sadness? Where was the hurt that I was experiencing? And it dawned on me. Oh….she is experiencing this officer's death the same way I experience the news story about the lady down the street who was murdered. I have no skin in the game. She was just another stranger. So, I got off the phone and called another friend who is married to a police officer, and we had a very deep, emotional discussion that was therapeutic for both of us.

She was very nice, and she was a good friend, but she did not relate to me in the way I needed sometimes. I am not saying that you cannot have non-police wife friends, but you have to understand that they aren't going to feel the same way that you do when you grieve the loss in the blue line family. And you must have someone that does. When we find out a cop has been killed, all of us hurt a little. I think we all see our husband's faces on those memorial pictures that float around Facebook. It is not the same as any other stranger being killed. The only time we can hear about a fatal car accident in another state on the other side of the country and feel strong emotions is when it involves a cop. This is a phenomenon only present in first responders. So, it is vital that we have someone that we can talk to and engage with in that way. Even our therapists can't do this, unless they are also married to a cop. That conversation I had with my police wife friend was truly needed at the time. I cannot imagine feeling that way and not having anyone to talk to about it that understands my seemingly misplaced sadness.

As police wives, we often deal with a lot of anxiety over whether or not our husbands will even make it back through the door in one piece, among other emotions such as frustration, and anger. It is important that we manage these emotions by adopting some relaxing coping strategies. Yoga, nature walks, bubble baths, reading, journaling, or meditating.

For me, it is painting. I admit, I am terrible at it. But it does relax me. One day, my friend said, "why don't you try meditating?" I laughed and said it wasn't for me. I am not the type of person to be able to sit still and do nothing but think about any one thing for any length of time. The idea of being idle is maddening to me. Then, one evening, I went to a paint night that my friend invited me to and it was the first time I ever touched a brush to canvas. I was so relaxed at the end of the night. I realized, hey! I meditated! Meditation is simply being mindful. And when I paint, I am mindful of every brush stroke. How would these trees look on a windy day? How would the sun reflect on these this lake? And that is all I am thinking about. What relaxes someone is different from person to person, but it's crucial to find your own ways to relax.

We also deal with a lot of strong, intense emotions, so it is important that we purge them sometimes. This is called, "catharsis."

Now, in my training, I always try to reference Vulcans in Star Trek. It never goes over well because no one ever admits they like Star Trek for some reason. I am still going to reference it here for fun. In Star Trek, there is an alien species called the Vulcans. On the outside, it would appear that Vulcans do not experience emotions. They are always, and only logical. However, the truth of it is that they have all the emotions, they just resist experiencing them. Only during "Kolinahr" do they experience emotions and purge them during their journey to embracing total logic. Experiencing strong emotions is a vital part of living. But we have to purge them at some point.

This is sometimes done by breaking things, throwing things, or other types of angry outbursts. There are healthier ways to do it; Screaming into a pillow or having a really good guttural cry works. You can also find hobbies that involve catharsis. I know a lot of wives have their own guns and go shooting sometimes. This is great! Kickboxing and high-intensity cardio are good options as well. I used to do karate with my son and found that kicking and punching those pads was very cathartic and relieving for me. It is also great exercise.

Some studies show that altruistic methods of coping have been found to be beneficial. If you are the type that gets a lift in your mood from seeing others benefit or by helping others achieve happiness, volunteer work may be a good option for you. A homeless shelter, or your church, perhaps.

Therapy, of course, is also an ideal coping strategy. The only distinction I make is that you ensure that you are doing individual therapy, and not necessarily marriage counseling. While I think marriage counseling is an excellent tool, I think that it is counterintuitive if you are dealing with your vicarious trauma resulting from helping your officer manage his mental health by bringing him to therapy to talk about it. I think it is important for both parties to have their own separate counselors.

I will stress again the importance of managing vicarious trauma. If you notice yourself exhibiting symptoms like irritability, your relationships suffering, impatience, exhaustion, rejecting physical and emotional closeness, loss of interest, or low motivation, these are signs that you need to take control of your emotions and behaviors and seek ways to manage your own mental health. You can't be good for your officer if you can't be good for yourself.

CHAPTER 11

CODE AND SCIP CRITICAL INCIDENT PROTOCOLS

Law enforcement spouses around the country are faced with the challenge of supporting their officers after a critical incident every day. Though every LEOW knows that their husband is walking into a dangerous situation on a daily basis, it is not uncommon for them to feel unprepared, confused, and helpless when their officer is involved in a traumatic event. I truly believe that we have all been there. I think any seasoned police wife would be lying if she said she has never found herself questioning how to best support her husband.

To combat this situation, I developed to critical incident protocols designed to work together or officers and their spouses. The first is CODE. This protocol is designed for the officer to have a step-by-step process of debriefing oneself after experiencing a traumatic event.

After you have been involved in a critical incident, stress management is a major factor in how you will heal moving forward. The CODE Critical Incident Protocol I developed helps officers break down stress management into four important steps with an easy to remember mnemonic.

Come Down

Open Communication

Down Time

Effort

The first step is to "come down," and involves the following measures

1. Decompression

   a. This looks different for each police officer. Some officers find this on their long commute home, others prefer to decompress by working out. Some like to sit down and watch tv, read, maybe even nap. This should take priority over everything else. Think of it as taking a moment to get your head together before you try to conquer everything else that is coming your way. Decompression happens before you jump into any other responsibilities or obligations. This is your transition from trauma to home.

2. Reduce Adrenaline

   a. Heightened adrenaline can lead to a wide variety of problems that make it difficult to cope and move past trauma. So, it is important to reduce and maintain a healthy level after you get home. This starts with decompression, but it can be easy to ramp it back up again with tv shows that depict high-intensity scenes. Cop shows, military shows, heavy action and adventure films, and anything that has a lot of loud noises, scary or startling scenes, and explosions or gunfire should really be avoided at this time.

3. Unplug

   a. It can be tempting after a critical incident to go on Facebook or turn on the TV to see what is being said about the event. This is especially true after a more controversial issue like an OIS with a racially charged element. But this will do you no good at all. There is absolutely nothing to gain from seeing how the media skews the facts, or to see what ignorant keyboard warriors, and armchair quarterbacks have to say about what happened. Further, it is too tempting to engage with people who don't care how educated you are or how intelligent your comment is. You can't argue with this ass-backwards knowledge. It is much better for your health to just not see it. It is easy to get wrapped up into and this is the worst time to do it.

4. Music and Laughter

   a. Cortisol is a stress hormone. Studies show that listening to music for 30 minutes will help to manage cortisol levels. And not only is it very difficult to be sad or mad when you are laughing, laughter also triggers the release of endorphins which decreases cortisol levels.

The second step is to "open communication."

1. Communicate with family, friends, and peers

   a. Studies show that supportive social interactions after a critical incident are vital in reducing an officer's vulnerability to PTSD and other mental health conditions. So, once you have come down from the intensity of the event, now is the time to seek out communication with your romantic partner, friends, family, and peers. This does not even necessarily mean you have to go into detail about what happened. The magic is in the support you naturally get from these people.

2. Explore departmental resources

   a. I encourage you to do this before you need it. however, it is very common for officers and their families to be unaware of either the fact that they have resources, or simply how to access them. Whatever the case, now is the time to become fluent in what resources your agency has to offer. Peer support, chaplains, the employee assistance program (EAP), and the staff psychologist are the most important and useful resources an officer has access to. All of these give you options of places you can go to communicate

3. Find a Mentor

   a. In my opinion, an officer involved in a critical incident should always be paired with an officer who has experienced it before. It can be an intense, and traumatizing experience for an officer. In my neck of the woods, there are "companion officers" who are specifically trained for this purpose. I had the pleasure of giving some training to them last year. Their job is to essentially hold the officer's hand through the entirety of the process. If your agency has something like this, I highly recommend taking advantage.

The third step is to invest in your "down time."

1. Facilitate Adequate Sleep

   a. You have read my chapter on sleep hygiene to learn why it is so important all of the time. But now it is especially important for the officer to get 7-9 hours of quality sleep. Sleep is a restorative process that is vital for clearing out the wear, tear, and trauma from the surface of the brain so that one can wake up and start fresh. It is also important in reducing stress and anxiety.

2. Quality Time

   a. It can be easy to get lost in the overall stress of the event. Don't forget to spend quality time with loved ones. Whether it be time that involves talking about the event or getting away from it completely. Make sure you carve out this time.

3. Fun

   a. Remember to have fun! It can be difficult to allow yourself that luxury in the midst of such an event, but you can't let yourself drown in the negativity.

4. Consider taking Extra Time off Work

   a. After administrative leave has expired, it may be a good idea to evaluate yourself and truly determine whether or not you could use a little more time to manage your stress. Don't let the pressure to return or the fear of repercussions cut into your healing. That extra time might mean the difference between coping with the trauma and developing a mental health concern.

The fourth and final step is to put in "effort"

1. Adopt Healthy Coping Strategies

   a. Ideally, an officer would have already learned to adopt healthy coping strategies. If not, now is the time to do it. In coming months, and possibly years, an officer can expect to experience a variety of stressful and intense moments from public outrage, to grand jury decisions, to civil trials, and just the process in general. It is vital that officers learn how to cope effectively to reduce the fallout from these events.

2. Consider seeing a Mental Health Professional Regularly

   a. While it isn't the most popular advice, it is one of the most helpful. Many officers will see the staff psychologist after a critical incident, but most won't continue seeing them. The benefits from long-term care can not only help you manage the stress from a single event, but it can help you develop tools to help manage the re-traumatization you will likely experience from all the events in the aftermath of a critical incident, especially those involving controversy.

3. Abstain from Alcohol for 30 days

   a. It is not uncommon for an officer to turn to alcohol as a coping strategy, even inadvertently. It is detrimental to one's ability to effectively and appropriately cope and is directly linked to PTSD. This is why I recommend abstaining from alcohol thirty days after a traumatic event to reduce your likelihood of developing a mental health condition.

After developing CODE, I felt that there should be a critical incident protocol for spouses as well. So came SCIP: The Spousal Critical Incident Protocol. This tool was designed to mirror the CODE protocol and serve two purposes. The spouse would have a systematic process to help the officer cope with trauma, as well as creating a process to manage her own stress.

When an officer returns home after being involved in a critical incident, he or she often faces a road to recovery. There are interviews, meetings, investigations, reliving of trauma, and re-traumatization. The romantic partner is the most stable, safest fixture in an officer's life. It is so important that the partner takes steps to help the officer manage and navigate the imminent stress the officer is going to face in the aftermath of a critical incident, such as an officer-involved shooting.

SCIP gives the partner four steps to follow to aid their officer:

Settle Down

Converse

Investigate

Perk-Up

The first step is to "settle down," and involves the following measures

1. Decompression

   a. This looks different for each police officer. But it is important for the spouse to understand that this time is absolutely, unequivocally vital after an officer has been involved in a traumatic incident. This is the officer's time to disengage from the ever-present work environment and experienced trauma, and transition to the comforts of the home. It must happen before the officer is expected to jump into the responsibilities and obligations of the home and family.

2. Reduce Adrenaline

   a. At this time, the spouse should work toward helping the officer reduce his adrenaline and maintain it at a healthy level. Avoid television shows with cop or military scenes, loud explosions, startling scenes, etc.

3. Unplug

   a. As a spouse, it can be tempting to research what your officer has been involved in, especially since he likely can't tell you all the details. But jumping on the TV or social media is one of the worst things you could do. First of all, nothing good will come of it. You can't trust anything the media says. There will *always* be people who have shit to talk. You will *never* change their minds if you engage. And you can get yourself in a lot of trouble. When you see something you don't like, and feel inclined to respond, not only can you get your officer in trouble, but you are also likely to draw unwanted and dangerous attention to yourself. So, put the phone away, turn off the TV, and just tend to your family.

4. Facilitate Adequate Sleep

   a. Sleep is always important for an officer, but now it is more important than ever. Now is the best time to put your sleep tricks to work. Bust out your essential oils, if you're into that sort of thing, draw the black-out curtains, turn on the white noise, tear up the honey-do list, and get him sleeping.

The second step is to "converse."

1. Be a cheerleader

   a. After a critical incident, there may be a lot of second-guessing. Now is a great time to reassure the officer that whatever happened, you're proud of him or her, you're there, and you're certain he did the right thing. Now is not the time to ask questions about the legitimacy of his or her thought process in taking whatever action. The officer's actions are going to be scrutinized and questioned by the administration, the court of public opinion, and possibly themselves. Your questions are not necessary here. But your reassurance and trust is vital.

2. Ask to be included

   a. Even if you have applied the principles on agreeing to be receptive and communicative from my training to your relationship, now is a good time to reiterate your intentions that you're here and that you want to be included. The officer may feel like now is a good time to lock up tight, or feel that he or she is protecting their partner by not talking about it. So, let the officer know that you're willing to listen. But don't push.

3. Ask, "what can I do?"

   a. I always encourage taking a preemptive strike against lack of preparedness, and much of this means to already have had a conversation about what the best things the partner can do for an officer in times of strong emotions or high stress. If this has not already happened, don't be afraid to ask, "what can I do for you?" This will obviously be different for every officer. It could be sleep, food, a hug, sex, space, or to talk.

The third step is to "investigate."

1. Explore Departmental Resources

   a. This is another area that I encourage spouses to do before an event like this happens, however, it is very common for officers and their families to be unaware of either the fact that they have resources, or simply how to access them. Whatever the case, now is the time to become fluent in what resources your officer's agency has to offer. Peer support, chaplains, the employee assistance program (EAP), and the staff psychologist are the most important and useful resources an officer has access to.

2. Find a Mentor

   a. In my opinion, an officer involved in a critical incident should always be paired with an officer who has experienced it before, and the same goes for the spouse. It can be an intense, and traumatizing experience for the spouse, just as much as the officer. Just like there are companion officers to hold the hand of the officers, there are also spouses of officers that do the same thing for the spouses whose husbands have been involved in a critical incident. If your officer's agency has something like this, I highly recommend taking advantage. If not, this might be a good time to get in touch with a wives group attached to your officer's agency, or maybe even reaching out on a social media group for spouses of officers.

The fourth and final step is to "perk-up"

1. Adopt Healthy Coping Strategies

   a. Ideally, an officer and romantic partner would have already learned to adopt healthy coping strategies. If not, now is the time to do it. In coming months, and possibly years, an officer and spouse can expect to experience a variety of stressful and intense moments from public outrage, to grand jury decisions, to civil trials, and just the process in general. It is vital that officers and spouses learn how to cope effectively to reduce the fallout from these events.

2. Laughter

   a. Not only is it really hard to be upset when you're laughing, it is actually triggering the release of endorphins, decreasing stress hormones and producing an overall sense of well-being. So rent a funny movie, pull up videos on you-tube, go to a stand-up comedy show, or even find elements of the event that one can draw some morbid humor from.

3. Quality Time

   a. It can be easy to get lost in the overall stress of the event. Don't forget to spend quality time together. Whether it be time that involves talking about the event, or getting away from it completely. Make sure you carve out time to spend together.

4. Fun

   a. Remember to have fun! It can be difficult to allow yourself that luxury in the midst of such an event, but you can't let yourself drown in the negativity. It benefits your officer for you to encourage fun and distract from the event.

5. Supportive peer interactions

   a. The study referenced earlier not only stated the crucial nature of romantic partner support, but also that of supportive interactions with peers.

No matter how loving and devoted the spouse is, she cannot relate to her officer the way other officers can. Make sure that the officer is able to touch base with his peers to talk, spend time together, or get support.

If you are a family going through this right now, I wish you the best of luck and truly hope my advice is helpful to you. If you are a reader that has yet to experience the aftermath of a critical incident, I hope that this helps you to prepare for the enormity of this fairly likely experience. Our officers depend on us, even if they don't know it.

CHAPTER 12

TACTICAL THINKING

In the current climate, it is already shaping up to be another awful year for police officers. We hear about officers being attacked and/or killed almost daily. So, what's the hardest thing about being married to a cop?

I met my husband in 2009, 11 years ago. That was a different time. Of course, it was always dangerous, but the sheer hatred and violence toward police officers simply was not as prevalent back then. So, while there was always a fear of losing my husband, there were just other things on my mind when answering that question. My biggest concerns fell somewhere between mandatory overtime and badge bunnies. Scheduling difficulties, missing holidays together, and weird hours were what bothered me the most. Of course, my fear of him becoming injured or killed was ever-present. But it was just...different.

Fast-forward to Ferguson when I think things really started going downhill. While I pride myself on good management of my anxiety in relation to my husband's job, it would be foolish to suggest that the rise in violence toward police does not make me uneasy. Every time another officer is murdered, it makes it a little harder for me to watch him walk out the door each day. Now, more than ever, it is vital that we have a way to manage our anxiety. I have said this so many times that it has become my slogan, "If you have to swallow half a bottle of Xanax every time your husband gets in a scuffle, you won't survive this lifestyle, and neither will your marriage."

But how do we do that when police officers are being killed left and right, often for no other reason than because they are police officers? Well, saying it is difficult is an understatement.

Awhile back, maybe 5 years ago it was about 9:00 am when the doorbell rang. I had yet to put on pants for the day, so I just decided to ignore it. About an hour later I heard of an officer-involved shooting on the news. It then dawned on me that I had not heard from my husband in a couple hours and I immediately thought, "Oh my God, what if that was a chaplain?" So, with a lump in my throat, I opened the door, praying there would be a package there. To my relief, there was. That was the day I realized I needed to find a way to get control of my nerves. (Also, it was the day I realized I really need to wear pants around the house on a regular basis.)

At that time, I was studying for my master's degree in psychology and I was learning about cognitive behavioral therapy (CBT). This is a therapeutic intervention and form of psychotherapy that essentially helps people learn how to change their thought processes to avoid becoming triggered by otherwise non-threatening stimuli. To understand CBT, I want to explain how cognition, or your thought processes work.

Cognition is a three-step process:

Step 1 is your input which comes from your external senses. It's the smell of meat cooking on a barbecue, the sound of a familiar song, or the texture of a fleece blanket as you run your fingers over it.

Step 2 is the process which is essentially all the thoughts that occur as a result of the input. Where does your mind go when you hear that or smell this? Does it make you nostalgic? Does it make you hungry?

Step 3 is the behavior that results after the processing of the information. After all that thinking, what happens on the outside? Do you cry? Laugh?

So, let's put it into the form of three examples:

You're walking down the streets of your hometown and you catch the scent of barbecuing meat (Input). You instantly feel the sensation of nostalgia You begin thinking about what this scent reminds you of. It takes you back to your childhood and you remember your dad standing in front of the grill every Sunday for dinner (Processing). This flood of fond memories of your dad, who perhaps has passed away recently causes you to cry (Behavior). We go through this three-step process many times throughout the day. For most people, most of the time, this is a fairly unremarkable event. But for people who have PTSD, for example, this can be what leads to panic attacks, flashbacks, or intrusive thoughts.

For example, let's say John is a police officer who suffers from PTSD from when he shot and killed someone who pulled a gun on him. John is walking down the street when he hears the sound of a car backfiring (Input). He instantly becomes alarmed as he is trying to identify the source of the sound. He suddenly remembers how much that sounded like when he pulled the trigger of his own gun to shoot that person. This is followed by memories of the shooting and how it played out (Processing). In his moment of fear, he becomes scared and takes cover behind a nearby vehicle (Behavior).

But my Tactical Thinking applies best to an example of an anxious police wife. I'm at home one day when Dan walks through the door. I immediately notice that he has, what appears to be a black eye. "What happened???" He says, "Oh I was just in a fight today." (Input).

...

My mind instantly starts racing. "What?! A fight?! OMG it could have been bad. You could have gotten hurt. You could have died. What would I do if you died? Oh God you're going to go to work tomorrow and what if you get into another fight?!" (Process). My anxiety gets the best of me and, thinking of him going to work tomorrow, I have a panic attack. (Behavior).

Tactical Thinking was designed specifically for police spouses to avoid their natural tendency to become nervous about their husband's job and redirect their thought processes away from a rabbit hole of anxious thoughts and toward more confidence and positivity. The key to this is becoming mindful of one's thought processes. Not necessarily just with respect to law enforcement issues, but with all thought processes in general.

Oftentimes, when we are lost in our own thoughts, we can go from thinking about something benign like, say, waffles one moment, and somehow start thinking about something totally unrelated like horses 5 minutes later, without being able to articulate how we got from point A to point B. This is because we typically are not mindful of our cognitive processes. Part of CBT is learning why and how our train of thought leaves one station and arrives in another. So, we walk it back. "I was thinking about horses because I was thinking about getting Maddox horseback-riding lessons. I was thinking about horseback-riding lessons because I felt like I needed to get him into an activity of some sort. I was thinking about activities because Maddox was having a freaking meltdown over soggy waffles. Working through that train of thought told me a little about how my thought processes work. And once I know how my thought processes work, I can have more control over where they go.

For example, after I had that bad car accident where I fell asleep and careened off the highway with my kids in tow, I was extremely nervous about driving. I noticed that I got particularly nervous when I was riding as a passenger with someone and their wheels crossed onto the annoying rumble strips, causing the car to vibrate obnoxiously. The sensation of the vibration (input) gave me butterflies. For a long time, I wasn't making the connection, but I would experience an intense feeling of dread and nervousness every time I felt it. One day I realized that those rumble strips are specifically to wake you up if you fell asleep at the wheel. That realization was the process. Even though sometimes you veer over onto them when you are not asleep, the connotation of the rumble strips alone led me to feel like I was about to be in an accident, and it would cause an anxious response (behavior).

Once I made that connection and was able to clearly identify my whole thought process, I stopped being so nervous when I accidently rolled over the rumble strips. Why is that? The answer is cliché, but "knowledge is power." When we understand why we feel something, we gain a sense of control that is therapeutic and vital in changing our thought processes. For many people with depression, PTSD, anxiety, and other mental illnesses, simply understanding where their thoughts came from or why they responded to something in a particular way goes a great distance in alleviating the symptoms of mental illness. This is why therapy is so important. Talking out loud and being guided through interpreting your thoughts and behaviors is essential for healing.

The key is first to learn how to be mindful of one's thought processes, to the extent where it becomes second nature to be aware of the train of thought. I know a therapist who gives her patients tape recorders and tasks them with walking around and thinking out loud: "I see a picture on the wall. It is of the ocean and there is a pirate ship. The pirate ship makes me think of the movie Pirates of the Caribbean. I love that movie. It is my favorite. It reminds me of that ride in Disneyland. That reminds me of the time I went with my dad. My dad is dead now. I miss him. Now I'm crying." It teaches them how to become more aware of how they get from point A to point B, while also teaching them how associations work.

The second step, if you will, is getting into the habit of gathering information.

One day, my husband came home from work with some pretty nasty scratches on his hand. I asked him what it was and, lo and behold, he had been in a pretty intense scuffle. The scuffle involved a knock-down, drag-out fight after the guy grabbed for my husband's gun. My immediate thought, of course, was a little fear and shock. But I made a point to stop and ask myself some questions. The first question was, "so he is standing in front of me right now. What does that tell me? Well, that he is safe, of course." So, there is no immediate need to become stressed out. Then my focus shifts to what information I need to turn this into something positive from which I can draw confidence. So, I tell him to tell me all the details. I want to know how it started, how it progressed and how it ended. What did he do to win the fight? Was he scared? What does the other guy look like? Maybe my husband is hella bad-ass. Where were your partners? Did they help? So, I can trust them to have your six?" All of these questions and thoughts lead to one important concept. He is here because he won the fight. He won the fight because he is skilled and good at his job. The fact that he is good at his job means that, tomorrow when he walks out the door, I can be a little more confident and a little less anxious as I wait for him to return. If we do not have this discussion, all it was, is another fight where he could have died.

It is also helpful to be aware of what you're doing that ramps up your anxiety. So, it is important to acknowledge cognitive distortions and flaws in your logic. A cognitive distortion is an irrational or exaggerated thought pattern that reinforces negativity. It is sometimes hard for us to see our own flaws, but it is crucial that we identify when we are experiencing cognitive distortions so that we can squash them before they eat away at us. It is also possible that, in gathering information to build confidence and positivity, we stumble upon information that is counter-productive. For example: Frank tells Susan that, in this case, his fill he asked for was very late getting to the scene, and had his back-up arrived more quickly, he would not have been in a fight at all. In this case, it is easy to rabbit hole yourself back to "OMG it could have been worse, he is lucky it wasn't worse because back up wasn't there, his partners are not good cops, he is going to die because his partners don't have his back." This is a cognitive distortion. Obviously, the fact that they were not there on time does not mean that they aren't good cops or that they don't have your husband's back. In this case, it is important that you address this flaw in your logic, remind yourself that this is probably not a common outcome, and ask questions to renew your positive outlook. "Why were they having trouble getting to you? Is this common? Is he usually trust-worthy? Etc. etc. Ultimately, the object is to gain a sense of control over your thought processes, refuse to let your anxiety get the best of you, and maintain a positive outlook on your officer's work in law enforcement.

Now, I am not suggesting that you should be able to start doing this today and be on top of your game tomorrow when your officer is in a fight. Again, CBT takes several months sometimes, and you can't be expected to master this right away. So, do not get discouraged if you have trouble with one step or another. Just learning to become mindful of your thought processes can be a long road. Any changes we make to habits and routines we have developed over 20 or 30 years take a big commitment and a lot of time. But you MUST get control of your anxiety or it will eat you alive in this lifestyle.

CHAPTER 13

WHY IS THIS IMPORTANT?

So, why are all these things important for your family? Well, simply and frankly, our officers are eating their guns at alarming rates. Officers are 3 times more likely to shoot themselves than they are to be shot by felons, according to the numbers in recent years. How do we stop this? I would say that it is our job as the romantic partner to listen, as well as the job of the officer to open up and address it. We are on the front lines of battling mental illness. As our officers' true partners, we are the ones who are charged with seeing the signs of mental illness and offering the care they need today. We could call ourselves first responders to our officers' trauma. They are not likely to go to a therapist, and even if they were, they are even more unlikely to be completely inclusive of all they are experiencing. When we married our partners, we vowed to be there in sickness and in health, and for better or for worse. This is the sickness, and this is the worse. We are the ones that promised that they could trust us and that we would be there for them. In a good marriage, with excellent communication, you may be the only one that can get the full picture from your officer. So, don't squander that gift.

Policing Stress on the Homefront © 2017 was designed upon my passionate belief that the battle against mental illness in cops has to be fought by a team of the officer and his romantic partner. It takes a partner who is willing to listen and do what they can to help the officer combat what is going on. It also takes an officer who will let them do that, which we will talk about in the next chapter. This is not easy, and it takes a significant sacrifice to allow yourself to process trauma along with your officer. That is not lost on me. But for a majority of law enforcement couples, the partner is the only one that can really discuss these concerns on the deep, intimate level that I believe is the most therapeutic and effective. The reason officers don't go to therapists is that they worry the concerns will get back to the administration and he or she will be terminated. Imagine going to a therapist and feeling uncomfortable with really expressing your strong emotions. What is the point? So, an officer needs to be able to find solace, trust, and sanctuary to be able to feel comfortable expressing emotions and talking. While counseling with a police psychologist is always going to be my professional recommendation, I admit sometimes it does not offer the 100% trustworthiness an officer may need to let go. If you are a romantic partner of an officer reading this, be that person. It is not easy, it exposes you to their trauma, but for some officers this is life and death.

It is so important that we realize that the risk of suicide in police officers is higher than that of being killed in the line of duty. Some see horrible things in their long career and just can't get the images out of their head. Others just lose themselves. We fawn over our officers and we worry about them at work. We wonder if a chaplain will show up at our door to tell us that something horrible has happened to them. But how many of us place the same concern on our officers' mental health? How many of us are watching for the signs? I think some of us have a tendency to place all of it on the job and think that, once they are home, they're safe. That is not always true. Do not become complacent to that.

CHAPTER 14

POSTTRAUMATIC STRESS DISORDER: THE SILENT KILLER

We have been throwing the acronym, PTSD around through every chapter. Let's talk about it a little more. We have talked about factors of it, we have talked about preventing it, but what we haven't really talked about is how our complacency contributes to it. No, I am not saying it is the spouse's fault or that there is responsibility there when there is a suicide. But how many spouses said, "I knew this was going to happen," when they found their officer dead by suicide? How many of you say, "Yeah, it's a problem, but not with *my* husband/wife."

Here is the truth, ladies and gentlemen, sometimes you just don't know simply because they just don't tell you. And it is so important for the spouse to consider this. I would be the first to suggest that my husband is not plagued by mental health issues. But I would be remiss to consider the fact that, despite my best efforts, he is holding something back. It is so incredibly common in police officers, that I must consider that I could miss something. We all must make this consideration.

So, what does it look like? Well, first we need to consider the first thirty days after a traumatic incident is often accompanied by symptoms that appear to be PTSD. These are what I call, "normal abnormal behaviors."

- Easily startled
- Withdrawal/Isolation
- Lack of interest in things that were once enjoyed
- Anxiety
- Panic attacks
- Nightmares
- Flashbacks
- Day intrusions (I just can't get the image out of my head)
- Other symptoms of depression

This is called Acute Stress Disorder. It is time to pay attention on day 1 of the first 30 days. This is a general number set by the American Psychiatric Association, of course, but this means the difference between ASD and PTSD. Also remember that PTSD can be the culmination of a number of common law enforcement stressors and general trauma exposure.

While I am not saying that a suicide is ever the spouse's fault. I am saying that part of our jobs as spouses should include maintaining a watchful eye and being vigilant about signs and symptoms of responses to repeated exposure to trauma. And sometimes, an officer by himself is not in tune with him or herself enough or is reluctant to seek help due to the stigma against help-seeking behavior. As partners, we really can be the first line of defense against the possible negative outcomes of PTSD, or even PTSD itself. So many widows of police officers who died by suicide have said, "there were no signs." There were, they just look different in officers and are often overlooked because the signs can be attributed to so many other things.

One thing I have noticed about working with law enforcement officers all over the country is that the common denominator that has no bounds is that help-seeking behavior is absolutely not normalized. It is a dirty word in EVERY police department. And sometimes, it slips by us in our homes. Some of you are reading this and think that your homes are safe places when they aren't. Some of you are reading this and think that, "well, he is a cop, he is used to this stuff." *you* may not be this person. But *someone*, maybe *many* are reading and saying just that. And society in general thinks that, because they are cops, trauma does not have an impact on their mental health. We forget that officers see things on a regular basis that we, as civilians, sometimes don't see in their entire lives. The average person experiences trauma one time in their life. I have been on over 80 ride-alongs at the time of this writing. I have seen 5 dead bodies in various states of decomposition, been in the same room as a newborn baby pulled out of a dumpster, and a mother who didn't seem to have any scruples about it. I have been in two pursuits, I've seen blood, brains, bullet holes, and I have seen someone die. This is via 800 hours over the course of 15 years. Imagine what an officer sees working 40 hours a week over the course of 20?

My point is this: Police officers are human, with human anatomy, and human brains. We were not designed to witness what they see on a regular basis. But all of us become complacent about it sometimes. I think that it is some sort of defense mechanism, however it's a dangerous one. It is dangerous for us to be unprepared and blind-sided when something terrible happens. And it is dangerous for our officers when they don't find a healthy, armed support system in their home. However, you take this thought, whether you think I am shifting blame or responsibility, or you are on the same page, PTSD is an enormous issue that we *all* fall short in battling. I'm just here to shed some light.

I think it is also important to consider how an officer's previous trauma outside of being a cop impacts his psychological resilience and ability to cope with trauma.

I think that most of us that are involved in the law enforcement community, be it by a career in law enforcement, being an avid supporter, or by being the loved one of a cop, share the idea that the general population tends to think of cops as machines. Machines that just materialize in their communities and start jamming people up for "no good reason." Then, at the end of the day, they vaporize and are never thought of again until the next time that person calls 911 or does something illegal. Cops are often objectified by people instead of thought of as humans just like them with their own lives, families, and hardships.

Through all my ride alongs, I have had the pleasure of meeting cops all over the country. I have had the privilege to, not only, see them do their jobs, but also to know them as people. A lot can happen in 10-12 hours spent in a patrol vehicle with a police officer. Rapports are built, walls come down, and I have the pleasure of seeing the human behind the badge. Not just, "I have a wife and two kids," rather, "I have a wife and two kids, so that child drowning call really bothered me." Not just, "I play golf on my free time," but, "I play golf on my free time to relax because I have been really stressed out lately." "I tried to save a kid who was shot, but EMS didn't get there in time, and I ended up watching him die. I couldn't sleep for days."

I think people don't realize how unrealistic their expectations of police officers' mental fortitude really are. "They're cops, they see it all the time. They are used to it."

People often use the word, "triggered." "I'm so triggered by what that person said." "You triggered me." But no one ever talks about how cops might be triggered by what they hear and see. Think for a second about something that triggers you. Let's say that you were sexually assaulted as a child, and one day you watch Law and Order and see a story about a child that was molested by her uncle in a fashion similar to your own circumstances. That would be triggering, right? It might bring back painful memories at least, or even launch you into a panic attack at worst.

Think about how much a cop might experience similar conditions. Since many of us tend to objectify cops as if they have no human feelings, thinking of an officer being "triggered" by something they happen upon during the course of their workday is not a thought that comes on naturally. Our first thought is often something to the effect of. "Oh, a dead body? I'm sure you see that all the time." We have expectations that cops aren't easily triggered. But we also experience triggers, and often make a point to avoid anything that would trigger us to begin with; a luxury cops don't have.

What we need to understand is that police officers, as soon as they hit the streets, are already at an increased risk of posttraumatic stress disorder (PTSD) and other mental illnesses. Their vulnerability to PTSD is dependent on a ton of various factors that are either helping or hindering factors such as the vulnerability of victims they come into contact with, scene reminders they are exposed to, level of emotional engagement they use to do their jobs, access to mental health resources, and even just various elements of their personalities. What is often overlooked is the presence of previous trauma exposure, or lack thereof. All of these factors impact an officer's resilience or vulnerability to PTSD. This means that previous trauma can increase an officer's likelihood of developing PTSD after being exposed to trauma at work. Many officers may even already have PTSD as a result of previous trauma exposure and can be heavily triggered by events they experience on the job or are in danger of increasing the severity of their condition.

I once was on a ride along with an officer whose mother abandoned him when he was very young. We responded to a call from a woman who said she was so fed up with her daughter that she wanted to drop her off at an adoption agency and leave her there. She wanted to know what was legally stopping her from doing so. Her intention was to leave her child there and never look back. As you can probably imagine, this brought up some painful memories for the officer who maintained his composure until he got back into the patrol vehicle and broke down.

On another ride-along, the officer I was with had found his father's body after he had hung himself when the officer was a teenager. When he was a rookie officer, he responded to a call of a suicide by hanging. He felt that, before he became a cop, he had coped with the event very well and had recovered from the trauma. However, when he responded to this call, it was incredibly painful and made him feel as though he had started all over. He has now found himself experiencing a particularly painful emotional response to any suicide or suicide attempt he has had to respond to in his long career.

A final example: An officer I rode with was a combat veteran well before he became a police officer. He had experienced a number of traumatic events while serving in Iraq involving gunfire, explosions, friends being killed, and being shot at. A few years after becoming a police officer, he was involved in a Hollywood-worthy shoot-out with several other officers. There were hundreds of rounds fired, suspects and hostages killed, vehicles struck by gunfire, and luck that he wasn't injured. Like the previous example, this officer did not feel as though he suffered from PTSD after his experiences in Iraq, however, the officer-involved shooting he experienced took him all the way back to his service in combat and he believes that he now suffers from PTSD.

In all these examples. We see officers who have an increased vulnerability to PTSD as a result of trauma suffered long before they became police officers. All three officers felt that they had coped and moved past what they had experienced in their younger years. Time healed, therapy was had (in one case), post-traumatic growth was achieved. But when they were hit with a triggering trauma, it was a totally different ball game.

One of the reasons this is the case, is Long Term Potentiation (LTP). This is the strengthening of the synapses that are responsible for communicating information from one neuron to the next. This happens all over the brain, but as it relates to trauma, I am talking about LTP occurring in the Hippocampus which is responsible for memory storage and recall. LTP is a double-edged sword, in that it can be great for helping us to make and store memories. But it also means we remember things we don't want to.

When we are repeatedly exposed to stimuli, the synapses in our brains are strengthened and more information is being transferred back and forth between neurons. This is good when we want to remember something like, how to spell a word or speak a foreign language. When we repeat a word over and over again, synapses are potentiated and the memory is stored. Likewise, when we experience trauma, and we are repeatedly exposed to it or related elements, the synapses are potentiated and the memory becomes solid and ever-present. So, when there is a previous trauma that has been stored away and is no longer in the forefront of our mind, and a reminder is forced, then potentiation occurs, strengthening the synapses, and bringing it all back.

So, bringing this back around to the officers I mentioned as examples, the common theme was the fact that the previous trauma was dealt with and placed comfortably in the past. These officers felt that the experiences, while traumatic and painful, were no longer impacting their daily lives. These were memories that were stored; present, but not pressing. Think of this as a two people that have discussed the event, but no longer talk about it with each other. They both know it's there, but it is no longer a topic of conversation.

Then the traumatic event happens at work, and the officer is reminded of the previous trauma. Now those two people have begun to discuss it again, and in intense fashion. As they discuss it with each other, more and more information is passing between the two: "Oh! And remember this happened too! And do you remember this part of the story and that part?" Now the two are both on board, frantically discussing this event and the whole memory is recalled. This is now coupled with a new memory and a new conversation. Now we have a new trauma that is attached to an old one. On top of that, more potentiation occurs with every inevitable step that occurs in the aftermath of a critical incident; The first interview where the officer has to recall what happened, the media response, the protests, the civil suit, the settlement, the anniversary, etc. Each of these events gets the two people started back on the conversation, which is attached to the old trauma that they are now talking about, yet again.

An officer that has moved beyond a traumatic event, unscathed by PTSD or other conditions, will now be more likely to develop PTSD after a traumatic event that triggers reminders of the previous one. Just like two people talking about an event more and more, ensuring that the information is present and powerful, the more an officer is repeatedly exposed to the same traumatic stimuli, the more an officer will maintain that powerful feeling of, "this just happened," and struggle to cope effectively.

I think that we really need to be mindful of the humanity of our police officers. I also think that most of the people that read my blogs already are, but hopefully this opens the eyes of some that aren't. They are humans just like us. They experience heartbreak, love, loss, joy, pain, disappointment, and despair. They have families that they would do anything for. They were innocent children once. They are loved by their mothers, fathers, sisters, brothers, and spouses. While a person they contact at work might hate a police officer for arresting them, or giving them a citation, there is someone or some people out there that think they hang the moon and love them unconditionally because they have had the privilege of seeing their good heart.

By this point in the book, I think you have gathered plenty of information about what PTSD is and what contributes to it. So, let's move on.

CHAPTER 15

HOW LAW ENFORCEMENT AGENCIES CAN NORMALIZING HELP- SEEKING BEHAVIOR

It is obviously not news to anyone that there is a stigma in police culture that presents a barrier to care for officers who could benefit from seeking help. But how to we address it? More specifically, how can law enforcement agencies address it?

First of all, why is this a problem to begin with?

The societal norms and expectations in the police culture are very long-standing. The cold and callous tough-guy attitude toward policing is alive and well and presents obstacles for officers who need help. In many parts of the country, these attitudes have not changed in the last 20 or 30 years. In others we are seeing a reach toward progressive measures to make a change. The latter are the agencies that bring me in to provide a unique mental health training. Either way, in every agency, there are officers, especially in command staff, that adhere to the old societal norms that you don't talk about mental illness, you suck it up and do your job. You will lose your gun and badge if you talk about that. This idea is what prevents officers from seeking help. The more these attitudes are held up, the less likely an officer is to mention a mental health concern, and the more likely they are to suffer in silence.

Law enforcement agencies inadvertently contribute to the mental health of their officers. There is something called the organizational justice theory that I always found interesting when studying law enforcement mental health. This theory suggests that employees of an organization are more likely to develop a mental illness if they perceive that the administration of that organization fails to tend to their well-being. We can apply this to a corporate office setting where employees are over-worked and underpaid, essentially. The employees that feel this is a picture of the administration's lack of care for their wellness are more likely to develop mental illness than their counterparts that feel their wellness is considered by their administration. If we apply this to the law enforcement population, you can imagine that, after all that is witnessed by a police officer, coupled with the cultural attitude that you are weak if you ask for help or even experience trauma, increases an officer's vulnerability to mental illness. This is compounded by the fact that there is already an increased risk of mental illness simply by being a police officer to begin with. There is a cycle that is perpetuated. Officers need help because of the nature of policing and culture, and the nature of policing and culture contributes to them needing help.

Why is this important?

Well, there were more than 200 in 2019 alone. Officers are three times more likely to die at their own hands than that of a felon. That is a pretty striking cause alone. But since it doesn't seem to be enough to get some agencies to change their ways, let's put it into a language that city administrations can understand:

Happy cops are productive cops. If you have a mentally unwell police force, what do you expect to gain from them? Proactive policing is more likely to happen when an officer is satisfied. Reactive policing is more effective when police officers like to do their job. Job satisfaction is linked with productivity in every industry. And that is not any different in terms of community policing. Let's go a step further:

What does productivity in police work translate to? I would argue that happier, more productive cops are going to be more effective cops. This doesn't necessarily mean that more arrests will be made, but perhaps there will. However, what I think is most important is that a happy cop is more likely to engage in aggressive proactive policing and be more enthusiastic when responding to crime. When there is a risk of serious death or injury to an officer just by getting out from behind the ballistic panels of their squad cars, and they aren't satisfied at their job, how can you expect them to be excited about going out of their way to do so? While they will run toward danger without a second thought when everyone else is running the other way to react to a crime, they may not be as likely to go the extra mile to be proactive. Further, I would go as far as suggesting that this would result in less citizen complaints. Happier cops have more stable and patient reactions to citizens they have contact with.

What does more effective policing mean? I would theorize that this translates to a lower crime rate and higher crime index. More criminals are taken off the street. Maybe recidivism is lower. Officers engage with the community more, and make it feel safer. Perhaps there is a faster response time. Ultimately, these mean a safer place to be. A safer place to live. And what does that mean? A safer place to live could mean higher property values, more people being willing to visit and live in the city, and a better economy. In a nutshell, I am arguing that, when officers' well-being is tended to, the economy of a city is better off. I don't think it is such a stretch.

So, what can an agency do?

This is all about fighting against and changing the police culture.

1. Start the conversation/raise awareness

   a. You have to start somewhere, and this is it. The agency needs to immediately take steps to break the stigma that comes with the police culture. This can be as simple as sending out a directive to officers that raises awareness to the steps the agency would like to pursue in order to break down the negative attitudes. And it can be as dramatic as bringing in a mental health professional and setting up a mandatory training for all officers, both in-service and academy level. "It's okay to not be okay" is the idea here.

2. Keep the conversation going

   a. It is not as simple as starting the conversation and raising awareness. If that happens and then nothing is done as a follow-up, the words and the efforts fall on deaf ears. An agency has to show that they are taking this seriously by keeping the conversation going. To me, this means by consistently taking steps to address mental illness. When one effort dies out, start another. Don't let it slip away and die.

3. Mental health initiatives/expansion on current mental health resources

   a. Pretty much all of my clients bring me in because they want to start a new chapter in their agency. I bring a new perspective that hasn't been seen before. So Policing Stress on the Homefront ©2017 is an agency's way to start something fresh and new after they have taken steps to raise awareness and support mental health to that point. Continuing to provide new ways to address mental illness is important for both addressing mental health concerns, as well as showing officers that the organization cares about their wellness.

4. Find influential cops to support the cause

    a. When I am training an agency to adopt Policing Stress on the Homefront ©2017, I always tell them to find their agency's Captain America. Every agency has one. They have the guy that everyone would follow to the gates of hell. It is the coolest guy in the agency, it's almost always a SWAT guy. He is the one you want to talk about your cause and let people know that it is okay to talk about mental health issues and that it is okay to have them.

5. Get admin visibly involved

    a. I talked about the organizational justice theory. The mental health initiatives are great, but they are even better when the command staff is visibly involved themselves. This shows the officers that the agency really does have a vested interest in their well-being.

6. Start a peer support network

    a. I work with a lot of agencies that have groups that are dedicated to responding to trauma or being available for officers who need to talk. Some officers will use this resource, others won't. But I think it is important to have the right people, with the right attitudes involved. Officers need to trust these peers, and know that what they say is not going to go beyond the circle of people they let in.

I truly believe that an agency who follows this advice and adopts these principles stands to benefit from a wide variety of changes simply by changing the police culture. A healthier force is a happier force. And a happier force is a more productive force.

Based on the interest I have in my training program, I know there are agencies that are looking to make this program a staple of their mental health provisions, or at least to find something new to apply to what they already have. These are agencies that are serious about mitigating the effects of repeated exposure to trauma by addressing concerns from all angles. Not only are they giving officers tons of valuable information on mental health, but they are involving the romantic partner and helping them learn how to be the best supporter they can be when an officer has experienced trauma. They aren't just piling them up with reading material, they are also helping families fortify their home to create the best environment for a police officer that they can when they leave work for the day.

More agencies need to take this into consideration. And more psychologists need to address this area of police psychology. Teach spouses how to communicate with their police officer partners. Help them find the resources their officers will need before they need them. Don't just send them home with books written for police officers. Do you know how hard it is to read and retain information when you're overwhelmed by everything it means to be married to a cop? Put them through real trainings where they can get hands-on experience and ask professionals important questions. Teach them the warning signs of alcoholism, suicide, and mental illness symptoms and teach them how to address them.

Remember earlier we talked about how 80% of police officers surveyed stated that the supportive social interactions with their romantic partners were critical for reducing vulnerability to PTSD. 80% is a huge number. This suggests that 8 out of 10 cops are saying that their romantic partner's support is vital. These are officers that are not talking to therapists, and likely not talking to their peers. Unfortunately, 80% is not reflective of the spouses who are not as open to listening as their officers are willing to talk. And often this is because they simply don't know how. So, where does that leave the officers that aren't talking to anyone?

We can do better. I'm pretty much an introvert from a small town in California where few people know who I am, short of the groomer I take my poodle to and the gal that does my nails. Yet, police departments all over the country are putting me on planes to come out and teach their officers and partners. What does that say about mental health provisions in law enforcement agencies? It means that I am bridging a very large gap, but that I am doing it by myself. The demand for my services is limited because involving spouses in mental health care is not on their radar.

Another caveat to the concept of normalizing help-seeking behavior is changing how we perceive mental illness.

Society has made it a dirty word. And it makes sense because generally, when society sees mental illness it is because they are witnessing it in all its ugliness when its inadequately treated or not treated at all. That guy getting arrested who was talking to himself and threatening to hurt himself is obviously not adequately medicated, if he has even been treated at all. Or that stressed out housewife with rambunctious kids that just had a very public nervous breakdown in the middle of the grocery store that never thought she had any valid reason to ask for help. Or that cop that was so scared to be labeled with PTSD that he didn't get help and ended up eating his gun.

But what would have happened if that crazy guy talking to himself on the street got his illness caught and treated in its early development? When he was given Thorazine to keep his psychotic episodes at bay?

John Nash was a mathematician and Nobel prize winner because he figured out how to function even with schizophrenia. That's because someone diagnosed him with something and gave the appropriate treatment. Did that diagnosis hold him back? Obviously not. Where would he be if he wasn't appropriately treated? Did you know Dr. Temple Grandin has Autism, yet revolutionized the cattle industry, and also how we treat autism. She had supportive people in her life that worked very hard and made sure that she made it somewhere not only *despite* her autism, but *because* of it.

People die every, single, day because of how society has made "mental disorder" such dirty words. Ensuring that people are afraid to ask for help because, OMG they might be labeled! Guess who was not labeled? A good chunk of those people you see at behavioral health who were picked up by police for having full conversations with their active auditory and visual hallucinations.

Guess who *was* labeled? Me. I have type 1 bipolar disorder. I'm on duloxetine, Latuda, Thorazine, Lamotrogine, and occasionally, lorazepam. But, I also have a PhD, and have already invented a training program that is being used in 16 states. And while most who know me probably think I'm a little weird, or awkward, I'm doing very well for myself. I got help because I knew something was wrong, I got therapy, and I was adequately medicated. It is difficult to admit that I have a mental disorder on a public forum but we *must* change the way we perceive mental illness and diagnoses. The diagnosis is what got me the right treatment recommendations. It's the only difference between me and that guy. For all we know that guy yelling non-sensical things at passers-by on the street has the potential to be a rocket scientist if only he was prescribed an antipsychotic and took it regularly.

Also, while I'm here...whoever you are reading this. I can nearly guarantee that you, too probably meet the diagnostic criteria for something in the Diagnostic and Statistical Manual of Mental Disorders. Anxiety, depression, PTSD, OCD, bipolar disorder, and maybe you're doing fine without having ever been diagnosed. So, who knows where you could be if mental illness wasn't so scary and you got the right treatment? Where would you be if you treated your depressive episode with anti-depressants like you treat the flu? Why is it hard to treat your obsessive-compulsive disorder with therapy, like you would treat your chronic back pain with physical therapy? And if you had cancer, you would get chemotherapy. How is it any different from getting cognitive behavioral therapy for PTSD? I believe this is a concept that needs to be clear to everyone attached to law enforcement in any way. And really, it should be normal for everyone.

None of you are "normal." Everyone is a little (or a lot) neurotic. And if you're saying that mental illness is something that should be hidden, masked, or ignored, then what are you saying about the people who suffer from it? This is my philosophy and my heart is set on spreading it so that officers will be afforded a more conducive environment for working in a job that requires repeated exposure to trauma.

CHAPTER 16

"CAN I GET MY OLD HUSBAND BACK?

Blog

No. No we can't. And let me tell you why…

Some of us married cops, and some us married men who became cops. Those of you who fall into the latter category can likely attest to the fact that your husband changed quite a bit over the course of time.

I met my husband when he had already been a cop for four years. But even I can honestly say that my husband is a bit different now than he was 5-10 years ago. I am sure the change is not as dramatic as those that were married before they joined the force.

I once was asked, "How do I get my old husband back?" My answer was, "You don't. You learn to accept your new one."

My studies in mental health in law enforcement have led me to the concept of repeated exposure to trauma, and how it impacts an officer's personality. Unlike the average person that experiences trauma once, twice, or a handful of times, an officer experiences in on a regular basis over the course of their whole career. On Monday, an officer might have to be exposed to human remains. On Tuesday he might see a person die while he is trying to revive them. On Wednesday he may be tasked with interviewing the victim of child molestation. On Thursday he might get shot at and be forced to shoot back. This would be an intense, unusually traumatic week for us. For an officer, having these types of weeks multiple times in a career is not unheard of. On top of the exposure to traumatic events, they are exposed to scene reminders of those traumatic events day in and day out. No officer is immune to experiencing trauma.

That being said, what does that do to someone's personality? What does it do to their behavior? We cannot expect our husbands to be the same man he was before he got into a job that caused him to experience trauma over, and over again.

Let's talk about Suzie. Suzie is a young adult woman who has led a pretty normal life. She grew up in a traditional family, got a good education, and for all intents and purposes, she had pretty average experiences. That is, until she was attacked and robbed at gunpoint in a dark alley as she walked home alone from work after dark. She was a confident person who did not see any harm in walking alone at night. She really had never experienced anything traumatic. But fears she never really even had were realized in this moment where she knew her life was in danger. Thankfully, all she physically lost was her wallet. But emotionally, she lost a chunk of her ability to function like the person she was before. Suzie no longer is comfortable walking alone at night. She suffers from anxiety in a variety of triggering situations that cause her to think of the event. She is more suspicious of people and certain situations. She has a tendency to be more aggressive in insisting that others are careful in how they get home in the evening. Her taste in men has changed from those who are taller and more muscular, to those who are closer to her stature. Her ignorance of the dangers is lost. She is now acutely aware that she is susceptible to attacks such as what she experienced, and she has changed in favor of someone who she believes is less vulnerable.

Now, let's talk about Jackie. Jackie had the same type of life before the exact same attack. After she has moved past the initial responses to trauma exposure, she goes and takes an intense self-defense class. She buys a gun and carries it everywhere. She still walks alone at night, not because she doesn't recognize the danger, but because she passionately refuses to let it get the best of her. She becomes more independent and less social with her friends, and she is absorbed in her efforts to avoid being vulnerable to anxiety and fear.

In both scenarios, both women came from a similar lifestyle and experienced similar trauma. But while each of the women took a different path on how they coped with trauma and moved forward, both women experienced a dramatic change in their personalites. This is after one traumatic event. This logic can be applied to rape victims, survivors of domestic violence, people who witnessed horrific events. None of them are the same after their one traumatic event. Are they?

So, we go back to police officers who have and will experience trauma over the course of 20 or 30 years. The average police officer has seen human remains, interviewed victims of child abuse, watched people die, witnessed the aftermath of horrific events, been in fear for their life, been in a fight, and a number of other things. The average civilian may have experienced one or two of these things in their lifetime. A police officer could honestly experience all these in one week. This repeats over the course of their career. So if we can expect a civilian who has been raped, or robbed at gun point, or seen someone murdered in front of their eyes to never be the same, we have to realize that police officers are experiencing a constant change in their personalities as well.

Even those of us who married cops have or will witness a shift in our husband's personality. We learn from our experiences each, and every time. Our brains develop methods of avoiding the experience again. That means that every time we experience trauma, we change the way we think.

Remember, we talked about the 3 steps of cognition: Input, process, and behavior. I want you to consider this using Suzie's example. Before Suzie was attacked, when she saw a dark alley way (external sense: Sight), she might have thought that it did not seem dangerous and it was the quickest route home (process), so she decides to venture through the alley (behavior). After the attack, she sees the same alley way, and while it is no different than before, her process has changed. Her external sense is the sight of the alley way. Her process consists of memories of the traumatic event, a realization that this route would be dangerous. And then her behavior is to turn around and find a new route. This is an unconscious shift in thought process. And the way we process our new thoughts leads to new behaviors. This becomes part of our personality.

So, a police officer who is repeatedly being exposed to trauma, is also repeatedly experiencing a shift in his thought process. As a result, his behavior is ever-changing. A rape victim can never go back to the woman she was before she was raped. No matter how well she adjusts, she will be different. Even if only to simply be more cautious about her decisions from now on. A survivor of domestic violence will invariably change with respect to her judgement of men and is likely going to be more choosy on who she gets comfortable and vulnerable with. If we expect our husbands to maintain the same personality that he had when you married him, we are setting ourselves and our marriages up for failure. This is part of the sacrifice of a police wife. We have to learn to continuously adapt.

One more personal story to illustrate this concept. When I was 19, I met a guy at my work. We will call him Leonard. I was pretty independent, confident, and adventurous. We hit it off really quickly and entered into a whirlwind romance. By the time he hit me the first time, we had already said our first "I love yous," considered our future together, and developed a co-dependent relationship. While he was completely financially dependent on my income, he got a tight grip on me and completely controlled my finances. He isolated me from my friends and family, and I experienced a great deal of gaslighting which kept me pretty faithful.

He got into the habit of hitting me when he was mad, and/or when he was drunk. Over time, my confidence broke down, I was scared all the time, and I couldn't go anywhere by myself. I finally got the guts to call 911 when he punched me in the side of the face while I was driving. That's when I was introduced to law enforcement.

Now, like many victims, I did go back to my abuser. But things got worse and by now I had developed a relationship with the sheriff's office and I soon had many people that helped me see what was going on. I eventually left him and never looked back. That does not mean I was the same woman I was before I met him. I was still no longer adventurous, independent, and confident. I was a little girl who was scared, having trouble fending for myself, and suffering from low self-esteem. I also lacked trust in men. When I was exposed to trauma, my cognitive processes changed. The biggest change was how I chose men moving forward. I looked for men that had attributes that were far removed from what I was used to. My brain felt this was a protective measure. I developed new parameters for my future partner without even putting in any thoughtful effort. Then look at me! I married a cop. Go figure.

The first time he hit me, my cognitive processes changed, and then every traumatic moment thereafter contributed to more changes, and more strengthening of the synapses which made it more traumatic. I assure you, I am not that scared little girl I was when I was 19 years old. Since then I have learned a lot, had a brief career in the military, spent years and years in college, dated and married different men, had children, and continue to experience even more all the time. This is all beyond the trauma I experienced as a child that, to this day, cause me to identify triggers and choices to avoid remembering it, getting into precarious situations, or putting my children in precarious positions. Those cognitive changes are key to both our personalities and our ability to thrive.

Police officers are no different. Every dead body they see. Every child molested by their uncle. Every physical altercation. These are all triggers for cognitive changes. This is the reason why your husband "changes" after he starts working as a police officer. This is why he lacks trust in what seems like it should be fine. It is why he scans the waistline of every stranger he finds himself in the same room with. And it is why he may have a tendency to be mean, authoritative, aggressive, or controlling when he may not have been before. Over time, he has learned that these are the typical qualities necessary for controlling and managing a volatile situation. It is extremely difficult to break those habits after they punch the clock. That being said, and leading me back to my point, the job has massive effects on the personality, and the personality plays a massive role in psychological resilience.

Dr. Jessica Burke, Ph.D.

So, keep this all in mind moving forward. Give him the benefit of the doubt that these personality changes aren't attributed to poor choices, to a loss of love, or empathy, or to your marriage. Work on accepting his ever-changing personality. Consider counseling to mitigate the effects of these changes. I am not saying to stay in the marriage and try to work it out if these changes involve domestic violence or substance abuse. But I am saying to consider cognitive changes when you want to accept that the person you married is simply not the same man, and that's okay.

CHAPTER 17

ACHIEVING INTIMACY IN AN OFFICER- INVOLVED MARRIAGE

Some will read this and say that the intimacy they have in their marriage is a.) already there with no help from me at all, or b.) their intimacy has nothing to do with him being a cop. And that's fine. But I do beg to differ on the latter.

The bottom line here is that law enforcement relationships are a whole different ball game from those that involve two regular people. (regular vs superheroes, of course). We struggle with a lot of difficult obstacles that other relationships simply don't encounter. Constantly worrying about the safety of our officers, often picking up the duties of the officer father or mother when they have to stay at work due to a stressful call, constantly being on the defensive either to protect oneself from hate or to vent our frustration with it, living with a person that is hypervigilant, helping our kids understand the dynamics of law enforcement, and why mommy or daddy cant' be home for Christmas. Further, these days, there is a constant nagging fear that one day our officers will have to take a life and face possible legal action.

We have to find a way to keep the healthy intimacy in our relationships. So, what is intimacy?

Sex?

That's the obvious answer, right? Well, I'm going to veer in a different direction. Not that sex isn't important for intimacy. It absolutely is. I, personally, believe that sexual intimacy is absolutely vital for a healthy romantic relationship of any kind. But there are so many other ways to achieve intimacy.

I have a very simple philosophy on how to achieve intimacy in a complicated relationship that involves repeated exposure to trauma. And it involves making the home a sanctuary in which our officers can recover from their traumatic, intense environments. We talked about this earlier, but the idea here is that, when we committed to a police officer, we vowed to be with them through sickness and in health, for better or for worse. So, at the end of the day I prepare for the blow, for the trauma. That is my job as a wife, no...as a partner. And yes, I don't love being exposed to the human nature he is exposed to. I don't love hearing about what dead bodies look like. And I don't love hearing about the shit parents that exist in the miserable city of Stockton. But the world doesn't revolve around me and my happiness. His need to have a safe space to talk is part of it too. And what does this have to do with intimacy? Well I think we forget that when our husbands signed on to the force, their job became part of them, part of their make-up, part of their identity, unlike most jobs. What they experience becomes part of how their brain works. What they do to stay alive at work goes with them everywhere. It is unrealistic to ask them to pretend they aren't a cop for your benefit. It's unhealthy, and its selfish to suggest they keep it to themselves. If you want a level of intimacy with your spouse beyond sex, it starts with being a true partner.

The very first step of this is to squash the "leave work at the door" mentality. This mentality is a sickness in law enforcement relationships. And because so many people try to take this route, police officers and other first responders think they should too. I think this mentality is okay when work is the same every day and does not require exposure to trauma, but not here.

Think about this. Let's go back to our friend Suzie. The one that was attacked on her way home from work, in case you have already forgotten her. Are we going to tell her to bottle it up, don't talk about it, leave it at the door? No. That is ridiculous, isn't it? She was traumatized! We are going to suggest that she open up about it. "I'm here if you want to talk," or we are going to suggest counseling for her. It is normal for us to suggest talking about things when someone has had a traumatic experience.

So why do so many law enforcement couples try to shut the reality out when the officer comes home from work? On an average day, he or she has been exposed to some form of trauma, some days being worse than others. Yes, we do the opposite of what we did for our friend, Suzie. We or they say, "you're home. It's time to shut it down. I don't want to talk about all that." It is important to note that I said, "we or they." I realize that sometimes it is the spouse that wants it to stay outside. And sometimes it is the officer that thinks that is the most appropriate way. But isn't it ridiculous that either one would come up with this idea when we put them next to Suzie?

I have said it in previous chapters, society has put a very unempathetic spin on what a police officer should be able to handle. We can't perpetuate that mentality. And as spouses, we often don't want to be reminded of the danger. So, it is so hard to drop this concept. This is understandable, but it is not healthy. Having open and honest communication, and a safe place to discuss trauma exposure is.

It is so important that we be our officers' most trusted allies. We all know that it is unlikely that he or she will seek therapy (But AWESOME if they do.) Talking to peers is fantastic, but the stigma is, unfortunately, alive and well, often preventing that. We, as blue line spouses are our officers' first line of defense against mental illness. As spouses, we strive to be their best friend, their soft place to fall, their safe space, there first confidant, and all that jazz. But too often, we miss the mark when it comes to discussing the darker side of law enforcement work. We don't want to talk about the gruesome details, the very real risk of death, the child victims, and all of that ugliness that lives in police work. But it is really part of being married to a cop.

If you are the wife that is reading this, shaking her head because "we have a rule, we never talk about work at home," you are exactly who I wrote this book for. If you are the one to refuse to talk about work, you are doing both your husband and yourself a disservice. While it is nice to feel like we live in a land of lollipops and cotton candy, the fact of the matter is, our husbands are going out every day and experiencing the worst of humanity. Every single call he responds to is something negative.

And day, after day, he is being repeatedly exposed to trauma. And not only is he regularly exposed to trauma, he also is dealing with factors that are proven to add to the cumulative nature of trauma such as poor work environment, continued exposure (like being held at the scene of human remains for a long time), long term potentiation (strengthening of the synapses in the brain when a person has to relive trauma), scene reminders, vulnerability of victims, and so many other stressors, on top of those that are not even related to work. If he isn't talking to a therapist, and he isn't talking to his peers, and he isn't able to talk to you, who is he talking to? There are two possible answers. 1.) Someone else is listening, or 2.) nobody, and his problems are eating him alive. Neither of these possibilities are good for us as spouses. We wouldn't ask our best friends to keep their trauma to themselves, we shouldn't ask our partners too either.

We have to understand that cops are cops at all times, and no matter how many times you insist, "no, they leave work at work," this is not reality. If he has ever seen a dead body, especially that of a baby or child, or watched someone die when he was there to help them. If he has ever been shot at, or had to draw his gun, or if he has ever had to fight for his life, or be told, "fuck the police" while he is there to do his job. Or if he has ever had a citizen complaint against him, or had to deal with the world's worst mother of the year who wanted to abandon their adopted child, then he is not leaving work at the door. I cannot promise this enough.

The officers also have an important role. While it should not be expected that you leave work at the door, I think it is also vital that you are cognizant of how you are transitioning, and how you're coming off at home. It is very difficult to be the partner of a cop. And it is made even more difficult when you take out the trauma of the day on your family, or when you take on an intimidating, controlling cop-like presence with your family. It is also impossible to be a partner through the thick, when you act like it is all in the thin. What I mean by that is, cops are notorious for experiencing trauma at work and walking in the door like they just had an uneventful day. It does no good for us to offer to carry your burdens, if you refuse to give them to us. And I think that you do that by trying to act like you are unscathed by even the worst of what you see at work. So, you walk in the door the same way an accountant probably walks through his. And we often figure, "it must have been a normal day. He would tell me if something crazy happened." But the fact is, you probably wouldn't. I think your first instinct is to pretend it is normal when you get home. I don't know if it's for your own benefit or for your spouse's, but if this is how you operate, consider how it is impacting your intimacy with your spouse. Let them be your partner.

Overtime often plays another role. I realize that mandatory OT is a thing. I realize sometimes you are expected to take overtime. But extra time away from your family can have a massive impact on your partnership. Extra hours at work reduce the amount of quality time you are getting with your family. On top of that, all that extra time may exhaust you and make it hard to spend quality time with your family. I always tell my husband, "When you work, I am working." What I mean is, if you're working, then I am parenting my kids by myself. I have two boys. A 7 year-old with autism and a 3 year-old that is a bully. So, sometimes it is hard to handle by myself. And while I don't necessarily have a problem with it, I think it's important for him to remember that when he is taking extra hours, he is signing me up for extra hours as well. In addition to that, he is reducing the hours that we can spend together as a family. That 8-hour shift he takes on Saturday is wiping out any plans I could have made for that day. So, while we always discuss voluntary overtime so there are no surprises, it still is a hindrance to getting adequate quality time together. So, we have to make sure that we are paying close attention to make up for that 8 hours spent at work when we are deciding what to do with our free time. I believe that it is crucial to make sure there is a healthy balance between overtime hours and quality time, with quality time tipping the scales.

Healthy communication is also very important for good intimacy. Refer to chapter 6 if you need a refresher on it. But beyond that, and more specifically, I think there are 7 conversations all couples in law enforcement should have:

1. Moments of pride:

   a. It is so important and vital in embracing this job in the home to pull out the positives, despite the fact that they are far outweighed by the negativity. Nevertheless, we have to try, and sometimes it is the hardest part of communication and team stress management. So, one conversation to have is any of those proud career moments. That time he saved a life, or he made a difference. The time his hands weren't tied, and he was able to help the helpless. You will know when it's time to have this conversation when he says things that suggest he is feeling pretty negative about his job. For example, California (where my husband is a cop) is becoming a much more dangerous and restrictive place to be a cop. He recently said, "I don't know if I even want to be a cop anymore." I very rarely hear that, but this is a good example of when it is time to remind them of why they became a cop in the first place. "So, tell me of a time you felt proud." This is when we have a talk about that one time he talked to this teenage gangbanger for a while and the kid actually said he was going to think about his suggestions. Our officers became cops for a reason. Very few of them do it for the money, right? So, revamp their passion for their jobs by reminding them that their good deeds rise above the negativity of the job. This is also a good way to bring the kids in when you talk about mommy or daddy's job.

2. Moments of happiness:

    a. The unfortunate truth is police officers aren't being dispatched to barbecues in their honor or a tree where he gets to save a kitten. Most of the time they are either going to bullshit calls that really never required police action, or because somebody was the victim of a crime. He is often dealing with people on one of the worst days of their lives. So, as a partner, it is great if we can take it upon ourselves to bring the happy moments, albeit fairly unusual, to the forefront of his mind. This could be that rare day when no one was rude and disrespectful to him for doing his job, when he was able to help a person who needed it, or when he got a pat on the back for good work.

3. Humorous moments:

   a. I don't know about you, but after being with a cop for ten years, and doing over 80 ride-alongs, I have come to prefer the dark humor over any other kind of humor. It's is a coping mechanism for them. Sometimes we hear them laugh or joke about things that normal humans would think are too morbid to be funny. I am sure for some it can come as a surprise and be uncomfortable, but I think you get used to it. I think that being able to pull the positives out of something negative is part of psychological resilience. And I believe that being able to laugh when you feel like crying is a survival mechanism for a cop.

4. Moments of fear:

   a. I once told my husband that I often felt uncomfortable with the fact that he always seemed so fearless. The fact that, yes, he would run into that burning building, or that he would approach a suspicious vehicle that he felt had a gun in it. He said, "You don't think I'm scared? Being scared is what keeps me alive." He was talking about the importance of resisting complacency and it was a relief to me. That brought up the conversation of times in his career when he felt fear. It is difficult to talk about and it requires a lot of trust in the partner, but it is so important to open-up about this with each other. This might be a specific event where something traumatic happened. It might be going to work the day after a shooting where five officers were taken in a brief moment by a sniper. Or it might have been his first day on the job, realizing his life could be on the line. We, as spouses need to be acutely aware of what they are experiencing when they walk out the door.

5. Moments of frustration:

a. One of the major peritraumatic factors in PTSD development is an officer's perception of an inability to help people. Many of our husbands joined the force to help people, but often they have limited resources, or the law ties their hands. Imagine the frustration of being asked to do a job, and then having all logical resources and abilities suspended. This is a component of stress that often gets left behind. So, discuss this and factor it into your stress management routines.

6. Moments of distress:

a. Distress is real psychological suffering and it can look different in each officer. And in each officer it can be triggered by different things. Let me bring up an example that is unconventional. I was watching that movie with Will Smith and the malfunctioning robots one night. It was the only thing on TV in my hotel room and I was feeling lazy. In it, Will Smith's character has a nightmare that we later realize is a memory of him being saved instead of the little girl he begged the robot to rescue. He wakes up, holds his gun to his head and says, "get out of there." I bring up this scene because it is so accurate. I believe that many suicides are likely preceded by a similar scene. Many officers with PTSD report experiencing intrusions which are basically waking nightmares. They are images that they can't get out of their head. It is the image of a person dying, a baby that passed from SIDS, or the muzzle fire from the barrel of their service weapon before they shot someone. I think officers are really good at coming home and letting us believe their day was normal. But we have to be on our toes. Get on top of what is causing your officer distress.

7. Things that cause stress:

  a. Another major peritraumatic factor is elements of the work environment that cause stress.

These could be your typical things commonly experienced by cops like malfunctioning equipment, poor relationships with peers and administrators, wondering how a citizen complaint will come out, or just sheer movement from call to call to call. To manage stress, we have to know what is causing it. And officers need to get it off their chest and understand where their own stress is coming from.

At the end of the day, the point is to open up a healthy line of communication and these are the things that are going to be most important to address. Like I have said many times in this book, spouses are the first line of defense against mental illnesses. Don't be afraid to talk about the deeper, darker sides of law enforcement.

We also have to be vigilant as spouses of law enforcement officers to the fact that we can't be selfish. But this is harder for a police spouse than it sounds.

Typically, when we enter into a relationship with any average person, there is a give and take that should be equal to both parties. Ideally, one is not more important than the other, and both should be willing to give of themselves to make the relationship work. But law enforcement relationships are anything but "typical." Specifically, one of the most significant atypical elements of a law enforcement relationship is the presence of repeated exposure to trauma in one party when it often is not in the other.

I think, by now, it would be redundant to harp on the fact that officers need support at home because they are traumatized. You get the picture. But what is important to realize is that it is easy to feel so exhausted by the end of the day that you don't want to expend any more energy. This is obviously understandable. But what often can happen is that you forget that your officer might need a lot of what's left to help him cope with what has happened. And it also may be used to hear about stuff that makes you even more emotionally exhausted or disturbed in some way.

This is part of the sacrifice that we make when we commit to a relationship with a police officer. But it is a sacrifice that seems to be missing from many of these relationships for a number of different reasons. I understand the idea of trying to safeguard the sanctity of your home by avoiding discussions about horrible things experienced on the job. But what is worse? Talking about dead bodies and child molesters? Or dealing with crippling mental illness and suicide? It does not serve our relationships to be selfish. We can't be too squeamish to hear about the blood and guts if they are causing our officers to be in distress. Be willing to put off your chores to lend your officer an ear. Tough it out if it means hearing about gruesome death and destruction. Interrupt your beauty sleep if he comes home in the middle of the night and he needs to talk. Hold off on talking about your stressful day if right now he needs to talk about the dead kid he saw. Cut your honey-do list in half if it is preventing him from getting adequate sleep. And suck it up and let him bring work home. It is wildly unrealistic to think that an officer can just shut it down because you can't handle the nature of the beast. You must be willing to make these sacrifices. Rest assured, if you aren't, this will be the downfall of your relationship.

Now if you as the spouse are also a first responder or are employed in a field that otherwise exposes you to trauma such as nursing or social work, then this does not really apply quite the same way. For example, if I am a nurse, it's conceivable that I, too, witnessed something similarly traumatic. In this case, I highly recommend something called, "collaborative therapy." In this type of therapeutic intervention, the officer has a therapist they meet with privately, the spouse has a therapist they meet with privately, and every so often all four meet and have a therapeutic session together. This way, the officer gets to discuss his trauma with someone, and so does the spouse. In their full inclusive session, they are able to learn how to navigate the fact that both are being repeatedly exposed to trauma and help them learn how to communicate. I should also note, I recommend this for all law enforcement couples, but I feel like it is a must for couples that both have jobs that require exposure to trauma.

Understand that I am not saying these sacrifices should come easily to you. And again, make no mistake, your mental health is equally important. But you must remember that, unless you, too, have a job wrought with trauma exposure, your mental health is likely in less danger and you have to prioritize communication accordingly. Do not interpret this as saying that you should not talk to your officer about what is weighing on you. You absolutely, 100% should. I am simply saying that there is a time and a place.

And while I said earlier that we are discussing intimacy beyond sex, I think I would be remiss to dismiss its importance in this discussion. Just like ensuring you have adequate quality time, one must ensure they have adequate sexual intimacy as well. I believe that there really is no better way to experience connectedness. I think that there is something really special about sex with your partner being something that is only between the two of you. (Unless of course you are polyamorous, I suppose) It's kind of like a secret handshake. It is the only way we share love with each other that can't be experienced by anyone else. And you are speaking a language that no one else understands because everyone's intimacy is different.

And it is the one and only time of the day that you are giving each other your undivided, unmatched attention and affection. No one is looking at their phone (I hope), no one is observing (unless you're an exhibitionist?), you are totally keyed in and giving your all to each other and it is unique from every other way in which we show each other love. So, when you are choosing what to do with that quality free time, always consider sex as an option. See? The doc said to have sex. Again, you're welcome.

That all being said, making sure that you're giving enough attention to sexual intimacy is as important as everything else I have discussed. But it is also one of the easiest things to let fall by the wayside. We get busy, we get tired, our schedules don't sync up, the kids get in the way, overtime happens, and a million other excuses. But that is what they are; excuses. Not only do they get in the way of connecting on an intimate level, it also often leads to a feeling of rejection for one party, which can also lead to resentment over time. That, in itself, is detrimental to intimacy with our partner.

CHAPTER 18

"BUT WHAT ABOUT THE KIDS?"

Here is the thing: A pretty well-known fact about me is that I do not, have not ever, and likely will never like kids that much. There came a time in my education where I said, "children? No. Not for me. Next!" My last child development class was 10 years ago. The one job I had where I worked with kids had me crying in the bathroom long enough for me to cool off, go back to group juvenile offender therapy, finish like a pro, and then I literally never went back. Forensic psychology, I'd argue, is as far away from child psychology as one can get, right?

That all being said, I do have two children that I am sort of attached to. My 7-year old is mildly autistic, and my 3-year old is right smack dab in the middle of his terrible threes. And I don't know if or what I am doing wrong. What I think I am doing right is finding a way to embrace my husband's job in the home, while tempering it for my young children's ears.

Our kids know that daddy is a police officer, or "pee-weese op-sir." And due to some shitty kids at day care, my son learned early that "daddy shoots bad guys." He was maybe 3 at the time and it disturbed me enough to send my husband in uniform to the day care to give a fun demonstration. He talked about gun safety, how to identify police officers, that they help, etc. And at home we talked to Maddox and explained the difference between a "bad boy" and a "bad guy" or criminal. This was also when Maddox got old enough to understand that people have guns and the reason daddy does too is because he could get shot at. Duncan, the 3-year old, could care less about the danger. But Maddox definitely has grasped that daddy is not completely safe at work.

So, we make a habit of talking to our kids about the good parts of law enforcement. At the dinner table, daddy might tell Maddox about the "vicious" chihuahua that jumped into his squad car other story Maddox would find amusing. I would also encourage my husband to make a point to bring up heart-warming true stories. Like a briefly lost child that he returned to his mommy. This never happened. But I am sure it is a good example for someone. I want my kids to see their daddy happy to do his job and make a difference. We don't have to give all the gory details, but we can decide what is appropriate as the kids get more mature. Kids are smart, and teenagers, though they are so obnoxious, often are capable of understanding the good and the bad of law enforcement without being traumatized.

I have been approached by parents that say, "we just tell johnny his dad is garbage truck driver." No. A thousand times no. This is like an ostrich burying his head in the sand as the predators circle. This idea is just going to break apart so quickly. Lying to your kids until an age they realize their parents have been lying to them is not what you're going for, unless you want to have no trust in your relationship moving forward. The second reason I disagree with this is because it is too easy for the kid to find out from other sources. Imagine your teenage daughter coming home saying that Shawn's mom told her that my dad put him in jail? Just be honest with your kids and find healthy coping strategies for them. Relaxing hobbies like yoga, cathartic like kickboxing, team sports, art. Read them books about cops and first responders. Show them funny movies like "Police Academy" or "21 Jump Street." Find ways to normalize the job, as well as to be realistic. They should know that his job is dangerous, but you can temper their fears by using positive language to express his place in his job. For example. "yes, daddy has a dangerous job, but your daddy is smart, he is a good cop, he has great friends for back up, and everything he does is to make sure he can get home to you."

I know there are kids that get bullied because their parents are cops. My opinion on this is to be honest with the child and let them make a decision on who they are going to tell. I would explain that there are a lot of people that don't agree with what cops do. Honestly, we know most cops are good, but there are a few cops that mess it up for everyone. And there are dumb people that are ignorant and who's logic can't be argued with. So, it may be best to withhold that from other kids. But it does not mean they have to have it all withheld from them as well. I hope that makes sense.

And my best advice for getting kids through this lifestyle is 2 things:

1. Routines work: I find kids are the most difficult to deal with when they are tired and/or hungry. So, it is an excellent idea to keep their sleep and eating times at a reasonable hour. In this lifestyle, a lot of changes happen, so we have to do our best to soften those blows to the kids. For example, when my husband goes to graves I am going to hate it. And it is going to mean a change to our schedule. When dad has his long weekends off are we going to change that? No. I am going to try my damn-dest

to keep my husband's sleep schedule on point, and the kids can work around that.

2. Don't miss opportunities for quality time: I am a big fan for spending all the quality time you can together. Cops are notorious for missing these opportunities. This is usually due to the nature of shift work, being tired, being mentally exhausted, feeling inundated with home projects. I get it. But that floorboard that needs replaced, that old motorcycle you're working on, the leaky faucet…. those won't matter. The wife isn't at home after her husband has been shot to death going, "Thank God he fixed that leaky faucet and old floorboard. Phew." But she might be looking at that floorboard thinking, "that was 2 hours we could have played catch with the kids outside."

Now I realize many cops have more than just a spouse, but also an ex…and more than one set of children. I believe this could add a new level of complexity. But my same suggestions stand. Work together as parents to make sure the kids have a healthy routine, even if that includes being picked up and switched around. And both parents need to maintain the honesty and transparency with their kids. If you are a cop or wife that is currently figuring out custodial arrangements, it is so important to not lose sight of how daddy or mommy being a cop makes this situation tougher. They are making a massive transition and often-times getting thrown from one extreme to the other. This is detrimental to a child's ability to grow and bloom.

Kids are smarter than us. They haven't been screwed up by the variety of things we have to endure to become an adult. If you don't let them adopt your unhealthy coping strategies, and you let them express themselves freely, you may be surprised at the choices they make and how they handle the fallout. Lying, hiding, or delaying the nature of the officer's job is doing nothing but setting you up for failure.

CHAPTER 19

THE ART OF BEING A POLICE WIFE

If you have been playing close attention, you may remember the comparison I made between the obsessive police wife and the crazy chicken lady. I was encouraging police wives to resist the urge to identify themselves totally and completely with being a police wife and only a police wife. I know that being married to cop is a badge of honor of sorts. We are proud of our heroes. I am proud of mine. And I brag about it every chance I get. I am kind of a hypocrite because my whole career is based on the foundation of being married to a cop. I get it. I take a lot of pride in being married to my hero, and you should too! It is just important to temper it with a flow outside of being married to a police officer.

Throughout my book, I have spent much of my time making jokes about my husband, focusing on the mental health needs of police officers, and not really making a point to talk about how proud of him I am. Oh! This man! In my heart, there is no man that could hold a candle to him. I love him even when I hate him. I love the way he kisses me. I love how he makes me laugh. I love the kind of father he is. He is my best friend, and sometimes he just makes my heart explode. I am so proud of the man he is, and especially the hero he is. His courage and strength amazes me to no end. Being married to him has made me feel so lucky. Sometimes he looks at me and I swoon thinking about how lucky I am that he chose me. He changed my life when he asked me to be his wife. But marrying a cop comes with unique changes and sacrifices.

Every morning at about 4:00 am, my Dan's obnoxious alarms start going off, and continue every ten minutes for the next 30-45 minutes. After he shuts it off and rolls out of bed, I fall back asleep only to be woken with a kiss on the cheek about 20 minutes later. I then always say, "I love you, be safe, have a good day." For 10 years, this, or some variation of this has been our routine. If I wake up and think, for some reason, that I didn't say those three things, I will call or text him to make sure. It has become a ritual of sorts, and I would not dare go a day without saying it.

I am sure that most couples are in the habit of kissing each other goodbye, but it means something very important to me, and to many of my fellow LEO wives, and I think it is often taken for granted by a lot of non-LEO couples; those that don't deal with a very real threat of death or serious injury on a regular basis. I know that if, God forbid, something happened to my husband on a day I failed to complete my ritual, I would take that regret to my grave.

I often see a meme float around Facebook that says, "You wouldn't understand unless the sound of Velcro makes you relax." For those that are unclear with this reference, it is talking about the common sound we hear when our husbands take off their Kevlar vests. It is a moment when we can breathe a sigh of relief and know they are home safe. That meme always reminds me how different my life became when I married my husband early in this law enforcement career. Something like the sound of Velcro, squeaky leather, or the zipper on his combat boots is more than just extraneous noise in the late or early hours. It is the sound of the gear that keeps him safe at work. The unnerving fact that he has to wear these every day is not lost on me. While I have become very good at managing my stress and anxiety, there are times when sending him to work is very difficult. The day after a sniper killed 5 Dallas, Texas officers was one of the most emotionally exhausting days of my marriage. And the sound of Velcro when he got home that day was remarkably soothing.

I have also learned what it is like to deeply mourn the loss of a stranger every 53 hours or so. Over the course of ten years, it has not gotten easier to learn about officers being lost in the line of duty. This is especially true when the officer is a motor like my husband, or when the officer is in the state of California. I think that, as members of the law enforcement family, most of us feel more upset by the deaths of police officers than most people do by the deaths of strangers. I think this is for two reasons. I think most of us see our husbands in the faces of these officers. And I think that we have a unique understanding of how tragic a police officer dying while serving his or her community really is. As spouses of police officers, we are able to get, at least, a glimpse of the camaraderie between officers, thankless work they do on a daily basis, the hard work they put in to get there, and the risk they face every day. Then we let our hearts walk around outside our body, risking their lives to provide for us, praying that they return home safely. And while many wives insist that they are free from worry, many others struggle with anxiety as a result of this unusual lifestyle.

Another change I have noticed is how much public perception of anything impacts my life. I pride myself on letting things roll off my back. I very rarely engage ignorance on social media. But there are some times where the court of public opinion rules on a law enforcement action and it completely screws up my day. I have 11 years of experience in this lifestyle, 4 years of dedicated study to mental health in law enforcement, 800 hours in a squad car on ride-alongs, and even a few months of military police academy training. When I see armchair quarterbacks posting on how they think police should have handled something, I pretty often am able to confidently decide whether or not they are remotely knowledgeable or realistic. I have learned that no matter how much training and study I have under my belt, I will never be able to change minds or productively argue with that logic. But when things heat up in the media about a controversial event, I feel frustrated and annoyed, both for myself, and for my husband who has to go to work with this population that is so hateful and disrespectful.

And then you have the common complaints of most police wives. We know better than to sit in a restaurant facing the door. We rarely can watch any type of law enforcement-related tv show or movie in peace. We find odd things like bullets, latex gloves, or remnants of notepads in the dryer. Clueless friends, family members, or neighbors often approach us wanting some form of legal advice. And we sometimes struggle with finding the right combination of laundry products to get blood and other bodily fluids out of our husbands' uniforms.

But I am going to be bold here and say that I am probably not the only one that complains about these oddities while secretly loving that they are part of my life. They are constant reminders that I married into a huge family of brave men and women that would put their life on the line to make a difference. They remind me that I was so lucky, that a brave, selfless, strong man like my husband chose me, of all people, to be his support system through all the trauma he is exposed to. I married my hero, and my life took a path that I believe only other police spouses can understand and embrace.

Sometimes, however, the changes can be harder to swallow than others.

Do you remember what your life was like before you met a cop and became embroiled in this lifestyle? Before you took a deep, uneasy breath as you watched him walk out the door every day? Before life was complicated by little things like where to sit in that restaurant, how to iron a uniform, or how to get that stink out of the vest cover? No, back even further. Do you remember what it was like before police officers were even something you thought of aside from how to avoid getting a speeding ticket?

I do. I was 25 when I met my husband. I had several years of an adult life where the only time I really thought about cops, aside from when I was in a violent relationship, was when I realized I passed one going 10 mph over. To be honest with you, if there was controversy, I never heard of it. It was insignificant to me. I didn't have any skin in the game. In fact, the last time I had a run in with a cop, I was speeding and got a ticket from a motorcycle cop in Stockton, California. Guess who that cop was? Who would have ever thought he and I would meet again and get married! Anyway…another story, for another day.

As I was scrolling through my Facebook feed one day, I was practically assaulted by post after post after post about a shooting in the neighboring county. I saw the body cam footage. My husband and I watched it together. My husband would have done the same thing those officers did. It makes perfect sense to me and it makes perfect sense to him. But the fact of the matter is that there is still a massive population to whom it does not make sense. As a result, there is anti-cop rhetoric all over places I frequent and wish I didn't have to see. It frustrates me. It makes me feel like my eyes are going to roll right out of my head. It makes me want to grab someone and shake them. Yet, there is not a thing I can do about it. Just like I think most wives do, I struggle with this. I want so badly to make people understand what they are missing. I want them to see the flaw in their logic. No this is not Hollywood where all cops are John Wayne, expert marksmen who can just wing someone or shoot a gun out of their hand. Tasers don't render people unconscious, especially not when they are on PCP or 6-feet tall and 300 lbs. But you can't argue with their ass-backwards logic. And it makes it that much more frustrating.

Sometimes I miss not having an opinion. Briefly seeing a news story involving controversial use of force and scrolling past to watch cute cat videos. I miss not worrying about the day my husband might be involved in a controversial shooting that will change our lives dramatically. And I often do briefly envy the wife who has a husband that has a normal 9 to 5 job that doesn't require a bulletproof vest. What would it be like if I had married a guy that wears a suit and tie, goes to work and, provided he doesn't get hit by a bus, comes home at the end of the day right in time for dinner? If I knew that, as long as he did his job the way he was supposed to, he wouldn't be faced with a decision that could very well get him all over the 6:00 news. And when the news came on about an officer-involved shooting, what it would be like to just shrug my shoulders and change the channel. In this alternate reality, I probably also wouldn't "like" so many cop pages and I wouldn't be constantly bombarded by vastly differing opinions on it either. How ignorant I was to this madness.

That all being said, I wouldn't trade my hero in for an accountant. I am immensely proud of my husband and everything he does to serve a community we don't even live in. I take pride in moments where it is safe to say, "My husband is a cop." I bask in those moments where

I am surrounded by people that I know recognize and appreciate my husband. And God knows I will never get sick of the uniform! But I do miss the lack of exhaustion over opinions that frustrate me to no end that I know I cannot do a damn thing to change. What has helped me over the years is choosing not to read Facebook comments, or at least refuse to engage. What has been even more helpful is immediately deleting any Facebook "friend" that posts anti-police rhetoric. No exceptions

So, hang in there, ladies. Things are extra frustrating right now. It may blow over, just in time for another shooting or police brutality claim. I'm afraid our police officers are at war, and it seems to be a war that is never-ending. I try not to get too political in my business, but we are fighting a losing battle with people that have the power to make our lives as law enforcement families that much more difficult. And to be honest, it terrifies me. I take pride in the fact that I built my business on my own sound mental health as a police wife. But I would be a liar if I said that I didn't experience anxiety sometimes over the climate. Not only do we send our husbands out the door in armor every day, but it seems like the world they go out into is getting darker every day.

In a previous chapter, I discussed the importance of having friends that are also married to cops. I talk about this in my classes and almost everywhere I go, there are wives that talk to me about their frustrations with the other wives they know. I'm going to be blunt here, and I don't think I will get a lot of kick back, police wives can be horrible, catty, gossipy, two-faced, jealous bitches. It's true. I have worked in 16 different states and I have yet to work with an agency that doesn't have problems with this.

Remember I mentioned my experience with the wives of my department that said they wanted this training but wanted someone else to teach it? Yeah. This is when I learned that there were snakes in the grass.

After that, things became more difficult for me. I had people gossip about me, start vicious rumors, challenge me on a public forum, unfriend me, and just generally poison the waters against me. I also witnessed other spouses being bullied, gossiped about, and spoken to in a condescending fashion.

When I walked away from the group and went out on my own, I started meeting wives from all over the country and discovered this nationwide phenomenon. In nearly every training, there was at least one wife that complained that she could not make friends with the wives at her husband's agency because they were rude, and catty. I have found that the police wife culture mirrors that of the police. We see bullying, gossip, rumors, cliques, and this weird idea that women wear their husband's rank and are better than the wives whose husbands have less time on. As a result, we get this high-school-ish feel when we think about spending time together as a family. Now, much like what we see in the police culture, while there are bullies and catty bitches, they will not hesitate to be there for you to help you pick up the pieces after a horrific loss, or to bring you lasagna when your husband suffers a work injury. Unfortunately, if you're not in the midst of trauma or misfortune, this is when they are most likely to be mean, rather than a friend. I am just being honest about what happens all over the country.

This negativity needs to stop. It serves no purpose other than to quench one's thirst for gossip and drama. As police wives, many of us struggle with depression and anxiety both as a result of commonality and prevalence of mental health issues in women, as well as the various struggles that come along with being married to a cop. So, why are we piling shit up on top of all that? Why are we making it worse for each other? We wear our pride over being a police wife like a badge of honor and that's great. We are all proud of our husbands and proud to be part of this family. But this behavior is unbecoming, and it really undermines our supportive intentions and goals. You can make all the casseroles you want and be the first to say, "I'm here if you need anything" to a struggling wife. But if you are condescending, catty, have a taste for gossip, and think you're better than everyone else because your husband has seniority, then that meal train you organized really isn't a genuine picture of your character and values, is it?

Being a police wife is a tough job, arguably one of the toughest. We often feel like single parents, we have to navigate holidays without our husbands, we are inundated with anti-police rhetoric non-stop, we kiss our husbands goodbye every day, knowing that it could be the last time. We feel sorrow for every cop that is killed in the line of duty. And we ALL experience these things. Your husband being a cop longer than mine does not make you better than me. If you see me slip up or make a mistake, you don't need to tell all the wives in your little "cool kids" clique. If you hear from your friend that I did something wrong, it isn't crucial that you let everybody else know about it. And believe it or not, it's not inappropriate to let me in on the rumor so I can squash it myself instead of blasting it out to all the other blabber-mouth bitches. You know, when a nasty rumor was spread around the department about me, I don't know how long it was floating around before another *officer in my husband's department* called me to tell me that he had heard it. That's how I found out. Not by the several other wives that heard it and manipulated it before me and allowed it to spread.

And if it sounds like I'm just ranting about how I was insulted. You're not wrong. I think what I have experienced is a really good example of what spouses all over the United States are dealing with from women that should be, and often pretend to be friends. And if I can use this platform to get through to the thousands of people that follow my blog by telling my story, perhaps I can make a small difference in the way we treat each other as part of this family. Those of you out there that know you are one of the snakes I talk about can count on the very people you bully to come to your aid if your husband is injured or, God forbid, killed. If you are married to a cop for any length of time, you can expect to need friends at some point, for any number of reasons.

We need each other. No one else quite understands what we deal with from one day to the next. No one else can relate to the unique emotional needs we have. Our non-police wife friends, bless their hearts, often have a hard time meeting those needs sheerly out of the struggle with understanding where we are coming from. Our LEOW friends are our biggest and best assets. No matter who you are and what a good police wife you are, whether you're married to a rookie or to a seasoned veteran, or whether you're an educated woman with a power career or a stay at home mom, we all have the same needs: reassurance, support, and understanding. There are a lot of us, so we don't need to try to do it alone. And that is why we have to promote a friendlier community. We are not going to get what we need from women that are married to plumbers. The wives of accountants aren't going to understand you and console you when you're a nervous wreck because your husband is at work during a mass casualty incident. The wife of a doctor may be able to give you some good advice on what flu remedy she uses with her kids, but will she get you when your officer is involved in a controversial shooting? Will the wife of a salesman be able to empathize when you are constantly missing your husband at kids' baseball games, school Christmas programs, or parties? Be kind to each other. You are all fighting battles that you need each other to win.

Now that that's off my chest…

CHAPTER 20

GOOD LUCK!

And here we are. You have reached the end of what amounts to 90 pages on a Word document. I hope that you have enjoyed the book and that it has offered some sort of benefit to your relationship.

We all have unique lives. It takes a special person to be a cop, and a special person to be married to one. Being a spouse of a cop is tough, but rewarding. Crazy, but lovely. Stressful, but exciting. I believe in my system and its principles. I truly believe that by applying my principles and philosophies that marriages can improve. I am not a perfect police wife. I fall short every day. But I believe that, by practicing what I preach, I have a healthy husband and a healthy marriage. I believe that these principles have had a significant impact on how our family deals with the trauma that is inevitable. I believe that there are so many wives out there that struggle with this life and can benefit by implementing just a couple of these changes. I believe it can save marriages. I believe it can save some officers from ending their own lives. And I believe that it can strengthen the intimate friendship that law enforcement families need to survive and thrive.

REFERENCE

American Psychiatric Association. (2013). *Diagnostic and statistical manual of mental disorders* (5ᵗʰ ed.). Arlington, VA: Author.

American Psychological Association. (2019). *The Road to Resilience.* Available: https://www.apa.org/helpcenter/road-resilience. Last accessed 4/24/2019.

Chopko, B A., Palmieri, P, A., Adams, R E.. (2015). Critical incident history questionnaire replication: Frequency and severity of trauma exposure among officers from small and midsize police agencies. *Journal of Traumatic Stress. 28 (2),* 157-161.

Conn, S M., Butterfield, L D.. (2013). Coping with secondary traumatic stress by general duty police officers practical implications. *Canadian Journal of Counseling & Psychotherapy. 47 (2),* 272-298.

Evans, R., Pistrang, N., Billings, J. (2013) Police officers' experiences of supportive and unsupportive social interactions following traumatic incidents, European

Journal of Psychotraumatology, 4:1, DOI: <u>10.3402/</u><u>ejpt.v4i0.19696</u>Fox et al

Fekedulegn, Desta, Burchfiel, Cecil M., Ma, Claudia C., Andrew, Michael E., Hartley, Tara A., Charles, Luenda E., Gu, Ja K., Violanti, John M.. (2017). Shift work and sleep quality among urban police officers. *Journal of Occupational and Environmental Medicine.* 58 (3), 66-71.

Officer Down Memorial Page. (2019). *Statistics.* Available: https://www.odmp.org/. Last accessed 4/24/2019.http://-www.policemag.com/channel/patrol/news/2018/04/20/140-officers-committed-suicide-in-2017.aspx

Sanctuary (n.d.) In *Merriam-Webster's collegiate dictionary.* Retrieved from http://www.merriam-webster.com/dictionary/sanctuary

Sharps. Matthew J. (2010). *Processing under Pressure: Stress, Memory, and Decision-Making.* 2nd ed. New York: Looseleaf Law . .

Violanti, J.M.. (2004). Predictors of police suicide ideation. *Suicide & Life Threatening Behavior. 34 (3),* 277-283.

ABOUT THE BOOK

Policing Stress on the Homefront was designed for police officers and the people who love them. This unique set of principles regards spouses and romantic partners as a critical component in mental health management. Learn how to mitigate the effects of repeated exposure to trauma as a partner, an officer, or as a team.

Printed in the United States
By Bookmasters